ABDELLATIF RAJI

The Human Journey

From Creation to Eternity — A Comprehensive Cosmic Vision

www.yaraak.com

To the seekers of light in times of darkness,
To those whose hearts are not satisfied by the glitter of this world,
To every soul that longs for its Creator,
And to all who have ever asked:
Who am I? Why was I created? Where am I headed?
To the readers who paused, reflected, and took a sincere step toward God,
I offer this work—
A quiet prayer,
A heartfelt invitation,
And a timeless reminder in an age of forgetfulness.

"Whoever knows himself, knows his Lord."
— Attributed to early Islamic sages

"And on the earth are signs for those with certainty— and in your own selves—do you not see?"
—Qur'an, Surah Adh-Dhariyat (51:20–21)

"The journey to God does not require feet, but hearts that remember the way."
— A contemporary reflection

Contents

IX   The Final Conclusion

Foreword

Throughout history, the human being has remained life's deepest question.

Who am I? Why was I created? Is my existence a fleeting coincidence—or part of a greater design? What ultimately awaits me at the end?

In a world racing forward—where distractions multiply and meaning fades—these questions shift from quiet reflection to an urgent inner cry. A cry that cannot be silenced by abstract theories or answered by knowledge divorced from divine guidance.

This book is an attempt to return the human being to the heart of that question—to open the door to a deeper understanding of the full human journey:

From the first spark of creation,

to the appearance of the soul in this world,

through every stage of existence—birth, life, death, the grave, resurrection, and judgment—

and finally, to the ultimate destiny: Paradise or Hell.

This is not merely a book of theology, nor a work of detached philosophy.

It is a call to meaning.

A map for conscious living.

A guide for the one walking toward God with insight.

It speaks to:

- the **mind** of the seeker,
- the **heart** of the traveler,
- the **soul** of the contemplative,
- and the **conscience** of anyone who still believes life carries a message.

Within these pages is a language that brings together:

- the precision of sacred knowledge,
- the beauty of spiritual reflection,
- and the weight of lived human experience.

The aim is not only to be read,
   but to be lived.
   A key to a path marked by faith, action, spiritual excellence (iḥsān), and the realization of life's highest purposes.
   To every living heart, every open mind, and every soul longing for truth—
   I dedicate this work.
   Not to add information,
   but to awaken meaning.

Preface

This book was not born from a desire to present conventional knowledge.
Rather, it emerged from an inner urgency—
a response to the silent questions rising in many hearts:
How can we understand ourselves?
How do we live in this world without being lost in it?
How do we link this fleeting life to the eternity that awaits?
It was written as a result of deep reflection on the complete human journey—
from creation to purpose to final destiny—
and from a sincere desire to rebuild both religious and existential awareness,
free from intellectual stagnation or rhetoric that fails to reach the weary human soul.
In this work, I have tried to bring together:

- **Doctrinal depth**, grounded in divine revelation,
- **Rational clarity**, attuned to the human disposition (fiṭrah),
- And a **spiritual method**, aimed at stirring the heart and awakening the conscience.

The journey unfolds through key stations of thought:

- God, creation, the universe, and the human being;
- Life, death, the grave, resurrection, and judgment;
- Paradise and Hell;
- The building blocks of Islam, faith (īmān), and excellence (iḥsān);

- The fulfillment of the higher objectives of the Shariah;
- And finally, the making of the complete human being—
- a soul at peace, and a force for good in the world.

This book does not claim to offer all the answers.
   Rather, it seeks to reopen the gates of the **great human questions**,
   and to serve as a conceptual and spiritual guide
   for those who wish to walk their path to God with awareness, sincerity,
and purpose.
   May it be:

- A spark of reflection in the heart of the seeker,
- A step toward transformation for the sincere soul,
- And a quiet companion in a noisy age.

God alone is the One who grants success and guides to the straight path.
   — Abdellatif Raji

Acknowledgments

Although this work appears under the name of a single author, in truth, it is the product of many hands, minds, and hearts. It reflects not only personal effort, but also the collective experiences—spiritual, intellectual, and human—that shaped its vision and direction.

First and foremost, all thanks and praise belong to God—Glorified and Exalted—who inspired this work, made its path smooth, and placed blessing in the time and intention behind it. To Him belongs all gratitude, in every beginning and every end.

I extend my heartfelt appreciation to:

- **My noble parents**, who nurtured in me the love of learning and the patience to pursue it with sincerity.
- **My teachers and mentors**, who taught me that true knowledge begins with self-awareness and blossoms through reverence for the Divine.
- **My friends and companions**, whose support, critique, and quiet encouragement helped carry this work through its most formative moments.
- **Every sincere reader**, whose reflections, questions, and presence reminded me that knowledge is a shared journey—not a solitary act.

And to every seeker striving for meaning in a distracted world—
I dedicate this effort to you.
May God accept it, make it a source of benefit and renewal, and allow it to reach the hearts that need it most.

Prologue

Since the dawn of his creation, man has been searching.

Searching for meaning,

for peace,

for a purpose beyond pleasure, utility, and the fleeting now.

In the noise of life, he may forget where he came from, why he is here, and where he is headed.

He may be distracted by the world's glitter, wearied by its questions, or suppress his inner voice out of fear of what it might reveal.

Yet a quiet voice persists—

rising from the depths of his innate nature, asking:

Is all this meaningless? Or is there a message behind this universe?

This book is not a ready-made answer,

nor a passing sermon—

it is the beginning of a journey.

A journey that begins with knowing God,

explores the mysteries of creation, the universe, and the human soul,

and traces the path from birth to beyond death—

through the grave, resurrection, and judgment—

to the final destiny: Paradise or Hell.

Along this path,

faith is cultivated,

actions are refined,

and spiritual excellence (iḥsān) is nurtured.

At its heart, this journey teaches how to fulfill the higher objectives of divine law

within oneself, the family, and society.

It is a journey inward with awareness,
a vision of the Hereafter with insight,
and a call to return to God with longing and responsibility.
Read this book not as a casual reader,
but as a traveler in search of his soul—
longing to know who he is, why he was created, and how he might be saved.

Welcome to the journey.

Introduction

1. Why This Book?

In our modern age—despite the advancement of science and technology—many people still do not know who they are, why they exist, or where they are ultimately headed.

They live without a map—torn between material distractions and inner unrest—detached from the greater truth behind the universe: that it is not random, and that every soul is part of a grand story that begins and ends with God.

This book offers a comprehensive vision of the complete human journey: its origin, purpose, mission, and final destiny.

2. What Is the Purpose of This Book?

This is not simply a study of creed or a guide to ritual worship.
It is a project of holistic formation:

- **Doctrinally** — To clarify faith and establish a unified worldview.
- **Spiritually** — To awaken the heart and connect it to its Creator.
- **Ethically** — To cultivate excellence (iḥsān) in character and behavior.
- **Culturally** — To revive awareness of the higher objectives of divine law (maqāṣid).
- **Existentially** — To illuminate the links between life and death, this world and the next, human freedom and divine will.

It is an invitation to rebuild the human being from within—and to let knowledge become a compass for conscious living.

3. What Is the Content of This Book?

The book is divided into seven interconnected parts, mapping the complete journey of the human soul:

1. **God, Creation, and the Universe** — Metaphysical foundations and cosmological reflection.
2. **The Human Being, Birth, and Life** — The station of vicegerency and moral trial.
3. **Death, the Grave, and the Barzakh** — The passage into the unseen.
4. **Resurrection and Judgment** — The moment of truth and eternal reckoning.
5. **Hell and Paradise** — The abodes of loss and everlasting bliss.
6. **The Complete Structure of Religion** — Islam, Faith (Īmān), and Excellence (Iḥsān).
7. **The Seven Higher Objectives of Sharia** — Preserving faith, life, intellect, family, wealth, homeland, and the ummah.

The final section links this journey to its ultimate meaning and asks the most vital question:

Will you live the life you were created for—or the life you've been distracted into?

4. Who Is This Book For?

This book speaks to:

- Every seeker of truth.
- Every soul wrestling with life's deepest questions.
- Every Muslim longing to worship God with clarity and depth.

- Every caller to faith seeking wisdom and renewal.
- Every sincere heart unsatisfied by the noise of materialism and the confusion of modernity.

5. How Should This Book Be Read?

Not all at once—but gradually, mindfully.

Read it with your heart before your intellect.

Let it stir reflection and action. Let it become a companion on your personal journey—not just to be studied, but lived.

6. A Final Word

When a person truly understands themselves,

they see life differently,

they act with purpose,

and they move from wandering in the margins to walking the center of their divine calling.

So begin here.

Let these pages be your first step:

toward God,

toward your true self,

toward your mission,

and toward the eternity that awaits.

I

General Introduction

*In a world marked by confusion and fragmentation, this book
presents a global vision grounded in the urgent human need to
understand our complete existential path—our origin, purpose,
and ultimate destiny. It calls for the integration of faith, reason,
and action as essential elements in restoring clarity and direction
to our lives. Rooted in both revelation and reflection, this work
offers not merely information but a transformative journey—one
that promises to accompany the reader through a unique blend
of spiritual insight and intellectual depth, toward a life of
meaning, awareness, and fulfillment.*

A Spiritual and Intellectual Guide to Life's Ultimate Purpose

Amid the clamor of modern life and the accelerating passage of time, the human being—when granted moments of clarity—asks:

Where did I come from? Why am I here? What is my ultimate destiny?

These are not abstract philosophical diversions. They are the core questions of existence.

From the moment of birth to the final breath, every human being is embarked on a divinely ordained journey—one shaped by moments of joy and sorrow, of seeking and understanding, of ignorance and awakening.

This book is both a spiritual invitation and an intellectual roadmap. It aims to accompany you on the most consequential journey a human being can undertake:

The journey of complete existence—from the first act of creation to the final return to eternity.

It is a journey that begins with the recognition of God—the Creator and Sustainer of all that exists—and culminates in an inevitable meeting with Him: a meeting marked either by eternal felicity or by enduring regret.

Together, we will explore the mysteries of creation and the intricate order of the cosmos. We will examine the human being as envisioned by the Divine: a morally responsible agent, endowed with free will, bearing profound accountability.

We will walk with you through the stages of life: the moment of birth, the struggle of worldly existence, and the solemn encounter with death. We will reflect on the solitude of the grave and the reality of **Barzakh**—the intermediate state between this world and the next, as understood in Islamic theology.

We will then witness the awe-inspiring resurrection, stand at the threshold of the Day of Judgment, and confront the ultimate destination: either **Paradise**, vast as the heavens and the earth, or **Hell**, whose fuel is people and stones.

Throughout this journey, we will demonstrate how the Five Pillars of Islam, the Six Pillars of Faith, and the highest spiritual station of **Ihsan** (excellence in worship and consciousness of God) are far more than religious practices. They are a comprehensive existential framework, guiding the soul toward meaning, purpose, and awakened living.

We will also illustrate how **Sharia**—the divine law—serves not merely as a legal system, but as a guardian of human flourishing. Its seven universal objectives—the protection of religion, life, intellect, lineage, wealth, homeland, and the **ummah** (community)—form the foundation for lasting well-being in both this life and the Hereafter.

This book is not just a text to be studied. It is a program for inner renewal, a call to live with intention, and an open invitation to every human being: to know oneself, to understand the meaning of life, and to walk with conviction toward eternal purpose.

Open your heart.

Prepare your mind.

Ready yourself for the greatest journey of all.

The human journey—from creation to eternity.

The Global Vision for Humanity's Need to Understand Its Complete Existential Path

Since the dawn of history, humanity has stood in awe before the profound mysteries of existence.

The great questions—**Where did I come from? Why am I here? Where am I going?**—have never been incidental curiosities. They form a persistent pulse within the conscience of every civilization, recurring across cultures, religions, and eras.

The human being is not merely a biological organism driven to eat, reproduce, and perish.

They are a rational, conscious entity—one who yearns for meaning as deeply as they yearn for air and water.

They seek the origin of their existence, long to understand their purpose, and tremble before the unknown future.

In the modern world—a world of speed, consumption, and accelerating technology, where screens often replace faces and attention is fragmented—the distance between human beings and their most essential questions has widened. Many now live as if life were a mechanical sequence: efficient, data-driven, yet devoid of higher purpose.

This estrangement from a comprehensive existential awareness is not a trivial loss. It is the root of widespread confusion, spiritual fatigue, and the deep psychological void afflicting millions today.

There arises, therefore, an urgent need for a project—both scientific and spiritual—that restores the human being to themselves. One that reopens the horizon of free thought and reconnects them to a reality beyond the material and the visible:

The reality of the complete path for which they were created.

- **Humanity's need to understand God**: for without knowledge of the Creator, one cannot truly know the self.
- **Humanity's need to understand creation and the universe**: for they form the stage on which consciousness, responsibility, and testing unfold.
- **Humanity's need to understand the self**: to discern its position, dignity, and moral responsibility.
- **Humanity's need to understand life, death, and the afterlife**: to live the present with full awareness of what lies ahead.
- **Humanity's need for a practical value system (Islam, Iman, Ihsan)**: to guide behavior and secure happiness in both this world and the next.
- **Humanity's need for protective objectives**: through the safe-guarding of religion, life, intellect, lineage, wealth, homeland, and community.

This comprehensive understanding of the human journey is not a philosophical luxury. It is a foundational requirement for achieving inner tranquility, behavioral integrity, and the renewal of both the individual and society.

Because the great revelations and divine teachings were revealed to establish this very awareness, reviving the complete existential path today is not merely a personal choice—

It is a collective obligation to rescue the human being from fragmentation, despair, and forgetfulness.

This book, therefore, is not addressed solely to Muslims or to the religious. It speaks to all people—wherever they may be—because it appeals to the shared human essence that longs for truth, grows through knowledge, and seeks lasting peace.

Let this scientific-spiritual journey mark a new beginning:

The birth of a human being who knows their truth, acts upon their destiny, and walks toward eternity with clarity, purpose, and peace.

Why Must We Understand Our Origin and Destiny?

The knowledge of one's origin and destiny is not a matter of intellectual curiosity or a passing philosophical inquiry—it is an existential necessity that speaks to the very core of what it means to be human.

A person unaware of where they come from lives a fragmented, aimless life—disconnected from any deeper sense of identity.

One who does not understand where they are headed stumbles through life without direction, like someone walking a path with no end or playing a game with no rules.

Understanding our origin answers the foundational questions of identity:

- Where did I come from?
- What is my relationship with the Creator?
- Why do I exist in this vast, ordered universe?

Understanding our destiny provides clarity of purpose:

- Where am I going?
- Does life end at death, or does something await beyond?
- How should I live today in light of my eternal future?

Those cut off from their origin become strangers to their own essence, often enslaved by illusions, appearances, and passing trends.

Those blind to their destiny chase hollow goals, follow distorted values, and often fall into moral confusion.

In contrast, awareness of both origin and destiny yields three vital outcomes:

1. **Realization of Life's True Meaning**
2. When a person knows they were created by a Wise and Intentional Creator, they live not under the illusion of randomness, but with clarity, humility, and purpose. Life becomes a trust, not a coincidence.
3. **Definition of Moral and Behavioral Responsibility**
4. A deep awareness of final accountability inspires one to act with integrity. It becomes a compass that steers choices toward justice, kindness, and meaningful contribution, and away from corruption and harm.
5. **Attainment of Spiritual Tranquility and Inner Peace**
6. The one who knows they are returning to a Merciful and Just Lord is not shaken by life's trials, nor seduced by its ornaments. Their peace comes not from circumstance, but from direction. They prepare for eternity with awareness and hope.

For this reason, the Qur'an repeatedly links the beginning of creation with the resurrection—reminding humanity that the origin and the end are inseparable truths. Only by grasping both can a person perceive life in a balanced and complete way.

Only then can they walk the path of true success—one that does not end at the grave, but stretches into everlasting reality.

Understanding our origin and destiny is not only the foundation of personal well-being—it is the beginning of a renewed human project:

- A human being whole in spirit and intellect
- A society rooted in faith, responsibility, and ethical vision
- A civilization awakened to the dignity of the human being as a moral, purposeful creature—not a transient material object

Those who do not know where they came from cannot know where they are going.

And those who are unaware of where they are headed cannot know how—or why—to begin the journey.

The Importance of Integrating Faith, Reason, and Action

True faith, enlightened reason, and righteous action form an inseparable triad in the comprehensive Islamic vision of humanity, the universe, and life.

❖ **Faith alone**, if left as a vague sentiment in the heart without the illumination of sound understanding, can devolve into blind emotion—vulnerable to extremism, superstition, or stagnation.

❖ **Reason alone**, if left to operate without the compass of divine revelation, risks becoming cold, reductionist, or arrogant—elevating materialism, falling into the delusions of hyper-rationalism, or collapsing under the weight of persistent doubt.

❖ **Action alone**, if detached from both inner conviction and thoughtful insight, may be reduced to mechanical habit or superficial ritual—devoid of sincerity, meaning, and transformative power in this life or the next.

For this reason, the divine message consistently calls for the integration of all three:

- **Faith** that fills the heart with certainty in God, His names, and His attributes.
- **Contemplative reason**, guided by ethical awareness, that reflects on the signs of God in the universe and within the self:

"Indeed, in the creation of the heavens and the earth and the alternation of the night and the day are signs for those of understanding."
(Qur'an, Āl 'Imrān 3:190)

- **Righteous action** that fulfills the purpose of worship and translates inner conviction into living behavior.

When integrated, faith, reason, and action yield:

- A **comprehensive understanding of existence**, harmonizing the inward and outward, the spiritual and material.
- A **moral framework** that protects the individual from ethical confusion and directs society toward justice and balance.
- A **civilizational vision** that unites scientific advancement with spiritual elevation and material development with moral clarity.

Faith nourishes the heart.
   Reason, when guided by revelation and humility, enlightens the mind.
   Action bears witness—before God, before the self, and before the world.
   There is no sincere faith without understanding,
   No sound reason without meaningful practice,
   And no accepted action without both intention and insight.
   Thus, humanity's journey—toward God and the highest realization of the self—cannot succeed without progressing along this balanced triadic path. Only by doing so can the human being be actualized in the noblest form of their existence.
   In a time marked by ideological confusion, unchecked materialism, and moral fragmentation, the integrated path of faith, reason, and action is not merely an ideal—it is the only road to true clarity, inner wholeness, and civilizational renewal.

The Promise to Accompany the Reader on a Unique Scientific–Spiritual Journey

In this book, we do not present a dry theoretical treatise, nor merely a historical overview of lofty ideas.

Rather, we invite you on a comprehensive journey—one that harmonizes rigorous inquiry with spiritual depth. A journey that reconnects you with your true self and opens your mind to horizons you may never have imagined.

This journey will be:

- **Scientific in its methodology**: grounded in evidence, shaped by reason, open to interdisciplinary insight, and directed at the conscious, thinking mind.
- **Spiritual in its purpose**: awakening the heart, stirring the innate disposition (*fitrah*), and inspiring excellence (*ihsan*) in your relationship with God, others, and the world.
- **Existential in its nature**: addressing your deepest questions with honesty and depth—never fleeing from inquiry, nor fearing the search for truth.

We will walk together, step by step:

- From the origin of existence to the final destiny.
- From knowing the Creator to understanding the self.

- From exploring the universe to preparing for the meeting with the One who created it.

You will be accompanied through essential stations:

- The emergence of creation, the unfolding of life, the reality of death, the solitude of the grave, the intermediate realm of *Barzakh* (the world between death and resurrection), the resurrection, the judgment, and the ultimate fate—Paradise or Hell.

Together, we will construct a clear framework of understanding through:

- The Five Pillars of Islam, the Six Pillars of Faith, the station of *Ihsan* (spiritual excellence), and the realization of the overarching purposes of *Sharia*—divine law aimed at preserving religion, life, intellect, lineage, wealth, and community.

Within the pages of this book, you will encounter:

- **An organized intellect** that lays firm methodological foundations.
- **A living heart** that responds to your need for serenity and inner peace.
- **An aspiring soul** that breaks the confines of worldly distraction and rises toward the eternal horizon.

This journey is not bound by time or place.
It is the journey of every human being who seeks truth,
Every mind that longs for wisdom,
Every soul that yearns for peace.
Join us on this path,
And allow your heart, your intellect, and your entire being
To bear witness to the most magnificent journey a human can undertake:
The Human Journey... From Creation to Eternity.

II

God, Creation, and the Universe — The Beginning of the Story

The journey begins with God, creation, and the universe—the foundational elements of the human story. God, in the Islamic and innate (fitrah) worldview, is the Absolute Truth, whose existence is affirmed through both rational and instinctive proofs. Creation marks the first divine act, carrying deep meaning and a purposeful philosophy that reveals the intentional design behind existence. The universe, in turn, unfolds as an open book of signs—an intricately ordered and precise system that not only reflects God's wisdom but also serves as a stage for human testing, inviting reflection, belief, and moral responsibility.

God, Creation, and the Universe as the Beginning of the Human Journey

Every great journey begins by returning to the source.

In the human journey toward self-discovery and ultimate destiny, the path must begin with God—

the origin of existence, the Creator of the universe, the Giver of life, and the source of all meaning.

Any attempt to understand existence without starting with the Creator is like trying to interpret a book without knowing its author, or navigating a vast map without a compass—disoriented and incomplete.

Therefore, in this part, we begin where all meaning begins:

- **God** — His existence, names, attributes, and His relationship with all that exists.
- **Creation** — The divine act that brought the universe into being with order, intention, and wisdom.
- **The Universe** — The open book that declares the majesty of the Creator through its beauty, structure, and laws. It is the first stage of human experience—and the arena of the great test.

Together, we will explore the answers to the timeless questions that stir every mind and heart:

- How can we come to know God through our intellect, our hearts, and our innate disposition (*fitrah*)?

- Why did God create? What is the purpose behind existence itself?
- How does the universe—with its vast galaxies, finely tuned laws, and profound mysteries—testify to the Creator's perfection?

This part lays the foundation for everything that follows.

Without a clear understanding of God and His attributes, of creation and its purpose, and of the universe and its harmony, we cannot build a coherent view of life, moral responsibility, or ultimate destiny.

This is the true beginning of the story:

- The story of a magnificent creation, designed with wisdom and care.
- The story of the human being—fashioned for a higher purpose and called to conscious living.
- The story of a universe waiting to be read by the eye of a seeker, guided by both faith and reason.

Let us prepare our minds for inquiry,
Let us ready our hearts for reflection,
And let us set out together—to the beginning of all things.

God — The Absolute Truth

Introduction

When the human being gazes into the vastness of the universe and reflects inward upon their own soul, a single truth reverberates beyond time:

There is a Great Creator—eternal, beyond all existence, behind every detail of this cosmos.

Faith in God's existence is not an inherited myth or cultural artifact. It is an innate, primordial certainty, deeply embedded within the human soul—manifest whenever the intellect is clear and the heart is unclouded.

Just as every effect reveals a cause, and every design implies a designer, the order, harmony, and precision of the universe point unmistakably to an Absolute Creator:

One who is bound by no limitations, resembles nothing in creation, and is never absent from any part of reality.

First: God — A Necessary Existence, Not a Contingent One

In rational philosophy, existence is categorized into two types:

- **Contingent existence**: beings that may or may not exist—such as trees, stars, animals, and humans. They depend on something outside themselves for their existence.
- **Necessary existence**: a being whose non-existence is impossible, whose existence is essential by its very nature, and who requires no cause to be brought into being.

God is the Necessary Existence.

His existence is a rational imperative—even before it is a religious one. All that exists draws its life, order, and continuity from Him.

He is the uncaused cause, the independent source of every dependent thing.

Thus, belief in God is the foundation of all other beliefs—giving coherence to our understanding of creation, life, morality, and ultimate destiny.

Second: God — Known Through His Names and Attributes

While reason affirms the reality of God's existence, it is revelation that allows us to know Him—personally, intimately, and meaningfully.

God has not left humanity in confusion or speculation. Through divine revelation, He has made Himself known by His majestic names and perfect attributes:

- **The Most Merciful** — whose mercy encompasses all things.
- **The Omnipotent** — for whom nothing is impossible.
- **The All-Knowing** — from whom nothing is hidden.

- **The Just** — who wrongs no one.
- **The Self-Sufficient** — who depends on no one and upon whom all depend.

Each of these names invites us to know, love, trust, and revere Him.

God is not an abstract concept or philosophical construct. He is the living reality—described by every excellence and free from every imperfection.

Third: God — The Source of Values and Meaning

When God is absent from a person's worldview, the foundations of morality and meaning begin to erode.

- Without God, life becomes a series of accidents—random, purposeless, and devoid of enduring significance.
- Without God, ethics collapse into relativism, and good and evil lose all objective grounding.
- Without God, humanity is reduced to biology—a mere organism striving for survival, not a soul striving for truth.

God is the One who infuses life with meaning, anchors morality in necessity, and gives coherence to the universe and our place within it.

This is why belief in God's existence is the first pillar of faith—and the key to every deeper truth.

Fourth: God — Present in Every Moment

Though God is the transcendent Creator—beyond time, space, and material constraint—He is also intimately near to His creation through His knowledge, will, mercy, and care.

He hears every call, sees every act, knows every secret:

- When you pray, it is He who listens and responds.
- When you grieve, it is He who knows the sorrow that words cannot express.
- When you strive in righteousness, it is He who sees and rewards your effort.

"And He is with you wherever you are."
  (Qur'an, Al-Ḥadīd 57:4)

This divine presence is the source of the profound peace and quiet confidence that believers carry within them—no matter what storms may rage outside.

Conclusion

God—the Absolute Truth—is the beginning of every inquiry and the end of every quest.

Through Him, life gains order, purpose, and clarity.

Without Him, the human being is lost in the labyrinths of confusion, chasing shadows in a world emptied of meaning.

Let us reflect deeply.

Let us open both our minds and our hearts to know God as He has revealed Himself.

And let us make faith in Him the light that illuminates every step of the journey ahead.

The Concept of God in the Islamic and Innate (Fitrah) Worldview

First: The Concept of God in the Islamic Worldview

In Islamic theology, God (*Allah*), exalted is He, is the One Absolute Reality—independent, eternal, and the foundation upon which all existence rests. Every created being depends on Him for its existence, provision, guidance, and ultimate purpose.

Islam does not merely affirm the existence of God as an abstract philosophical conclusion. Rather, it offers a complete, integrated understanding of His **essence**, **names**, **attributes**, and **actions**—a conception that transcends all imperfection and elevates God to the pinnacle of absolute perfection.

Islam asserts that God:

- Is **One without partner**—in His essence, names, attributes, and actions.
- Is the **Creator of all things**—utterly self-sufficient, while all creation depends on Him entirely.
- Possesses **complete attributes**—perfection in knowledge, power, will, wisdom, justice, mercy, and majesty.
- Is **transcendent beyond comparison or likeness**:

31

> *"There is nothing like unto Him, and He is the All-Hearing, the All-Seeing."*
> (Qur'an, Ash-Shūra 42:11)

In Islam, God is not a distant force nor a vague cosmic energy.

He is the **Living, Sustaining** Lord—who acts with will and wisdom, governs with mercy and justice, and interacts with creation through **revelation, legislation, decree,** and **destiny**.

He invites humanity to know Him, love Him, and worship Him—out of free will, not compulsion.

Second: The Concept of God in the Innate (Fitrah) Worldview

The pure human *fitrah*—before being obscured by doubt or distorted by external influence—naturally and intuitively recognizes the existence of God.

- Every human being senses that the universe must have a Wise and Intentional Creator.
- Every soul instinctively turns to God in moments of fear, helplessness, and desperation—without training or instruction.
- Children, prior to environmental conditioning, naturally incline toward belief in a Supreme Being.

This intuitive awareness is affirmed in the words of the Prophet Muhammad (peace be upon him):

> "Every child is born upon the natural disposition (fitrah), but his parents make him a Jew, a Christian, or a Magian."
> (Narrated by al-Bukhari and Muslim)

Classical scholars such as **Ibn Taymiyyah, al-Ghazālī**, and **Ibn 'Ashūr** held that the *fitrah* includes not only an innate recognition of God's existence, but also a basic moral orientation toward truth and goodness.

Thus, the *fitrah* is not neutral—it is actively predisposed toward monotheism (*tawḥīd*), reverence for the Creator, and an inner yearning for transcendence.

Accordingly, the *fitrah* aligns naturally with the Islamic view of God:

- Both affirm God as the Creator and Sustainer.
- Both uphold the oneness of God.
- Both reject any imperfection, weakness, or dependency attributed to Him.

Third: The Integration of the Islamic and Innate Perspectives

Islam does not negate the role of *fitrah* or reason in knowing God. Rather, it integrates them and elevates their potential through the guidance of divine revelation.

- The *fitrah* plants the seed of intuitive recognition and spiritual longing.
- The intellect provides rational proof and philosophical coherence.
- Revelation (the Qur'an and Sunnah) completes the picture—guiding the heart and mind toward a perfected understanding of the Divine.

Thus, the Islamic conception of God rests on three complementary foundations:

1. **Sound innate disposition** (*fitrah*)
2. **Sound reasoning** ('*aql*)
3. **Authentic revelation** (*waḥy*)

33

Through this integration, the human being attains a **balanced knowledge of God**—one that is emotional, intellectual, and practical.

This leads to:

- Firm and enlightened faith
- Sincere worship and servitude
- A purposeful journey toward the ultimate aim of existence

Conclusion

The Islamic worldview presents a conception of God that is rooted in both reason and revelation, while also echoing the deepest voice within the human soul.

It does not ask the human being to silence the mind or suppress the heart; rather, it calls them to awaken both—unifying the internal voice of the *fitrah*, the rational clarity of the intellect, and the illuminating guidance of divine revelation.

In this harmony, faith is no longer a blind leap, but a conscious return to what we were always meant to know.

Such a vision offers not only theological truth but existential coherence—anchoring values, grounding purpose, and guiding the human being across all times and cultures toward their true Creator.

Rational and Innate Proofs for the Existence of God

Faith in the existence of God is not grounded in vague emotion or inherited tradition alone. Rather, it is a conviction rooted in the strongest foundations of **sound reason** and **pure innate disposition** (*fitrah*).

Islamic revelation and clear human intellect both affirm God's existence through multiple, complementary lines of evidence—each reinforcing the other and leading the sincere seeker to certainty.

First: Rational Proofs

1. The Argument from Contingent Existence (Proof of Creation and Origination)

- Everything within the universe is **contingent**—it exists, but it could have just as easily not existed. It is dependent, finite, and subject to change.
- It is impossible for contingent things to arise from absolute nothingness, or to explain themselves by themselves.
- Therefore, the existence of this world points necessarily to a **non-contingent**, eternal being: a **Necessary Existence** who brought all things into being without Himself being brought into being.

This argument, classically articulated by scholars such as Ibn Sīnā and developed

35

further in kalām theology, affirms that the universe requires a cause that is independent, eternal, and self-sufficient—namely, God.

2. The Argument from Design and Order (Teleological Proof)

- The universe is governed by stunning precision and balance—from the structure of atoms to the rotation of galaxies.
- Such coherence and purposeful order cannot arise by chance. Order implies intent, design, and intelligent causation.

"The handiwork of Allah, who perfected all things."
(Qur'an, An-Naml 27:88)

- This vast, integrated system reflects the will of a **wise, all-powerful** Creator who designed and sustains it.

3. The Argument from Causality (Proof of the First Cause)

- Every effect has a cause. This causal chain cannot extend infinitely backward—because if every cause required a prior cause, nothing would ever begin.
- Therefore, the chain must terminate at a **First Cause**—uncaused, eternal, and independent.

This reasoning, affirmed by theologians like al-Ghazālī and philosophers like Aristotle, leads to the conclusion that there must be a Prime Mover—one who initiates all causes without being caused.

4. The Argument from Purpose and Intention

- From the flight of birds to the human immune system, natural processes are goal-directed and purposeful.
- This teleological behavior implies intention—a deliberate will directing things toward ends.
- Such directedness cannot originate from inanimate matter or unconscious processes. It points to a **conscious, wise Creator** who designed life with meaning and purpose.

Second: Innate (Fitrah) Proofs

1. The Inner Awareness of the Creator

- Every human being, at the core of their soul, senses the existence of a Supreme Power above them—near, aware, and in control.
- This awareness does not require philosophical training or religious education. It arises naturally from the uncorrupted *fitrah*—the primordial disposition upon which God created humanity.

2. Spontaneous Turning to God in Crisis

- In moments of fear, desperation, or helplessness—when all worldly means fail—human beings instinctively turn upward, calling upon a Higher Power.

"And when they board a ship, they supplicate Allah, sincere to Him in religion."
  (Qur'an, Al-ʿAnkabūt 29:65)

- This instinctive turning, across cultures and times, reflects an embedded certainty of God's reality.

3. Spiritual Tranquility in the Remembrance of God

- The human heart finds peace and grounding in connection with the Divine—and feels unease and emptiness in His absence.

"Indeed, by the remembrance of Allah do hearts find rest."
  (Qur'an, Ar-Ra'd 13:28)

- This deep inner resonance affirms that the soul was designed to know, love, and rely upon its Creator.

Conclusion

Rational and innate proofs for God's existence do not oppose one another—they converge in harmony:

- Reason affirms the necessity of a wise, eternal Creator.
- The *fitrah* rejoices in His nearness and finds peace in His remembrance.

To deny God is not simply a theological error—it is a rupture from the human soul's deepest truth, and a departure from the very logic upon which our understanding of existence depends.

God is the most certain of all truths—more evident than denial, more stable than doubt, and nearer to the human being than their own breath.

Creation — The First Act

Introduction

When we lift our eyes to the sky, observe the intricate design of our bodies, or reflect on the birth and development of life, we intuitively and rationally recognize a profound truth:

This world did not emerge by chance, nor did it create itself. It came into existence by the will of a Wise, All-Knowing, and All-Powerful Creator.

The act of creation is the first visible manifestation of God's will, knowledge, and power— the foundation upon which all existence, seen and unseen, is built.

Creation is not a distant event buried in the past;

it is a continuous, ever-renewed act of divine command:

> *"But they are in confusion over a new creation."*
> *(Qur'an, Qāf 50:15)*

First: The Concept of Creation in the Islamic Worldview

In Islam, creation is defined as:

- The bringing of existence out of **absolute nonexistence**, solely by the will of God (*Allah*)—without the use of pre-existing material or external cause.
- The origination of all the foundations of reality: **time, space, matter, energy, life, intellect, and soul**.

As Allah states:

> *"Allah is the Creator of all things, and He is, over all things, Disposer of affairs."*
> (Qur'an, Az-Zumar 39:62)

Creation is a divine act that is:

- **Exclusive to God**—no one shares in it, rivals it, or assists in it.
- **Free of need**—God does not require help, raw material, or cause to bring about His will.
- **Intentional and wise**—not a blind accident or mechanical process, but a purposeful, deliberate act guided by infinite wisdom.

This concept contrasts with ancient myths and materialist philosophies that suggest creation emerged from chaos, necessity, or self-organization. In Islam, creation stems from conscious, divine volition—*"Be, and it is."*

Second: The Purpose of Creation

Why did God create the universe? Why were human beings brought into existence?

The Qur'an answers this question with clarity:

> *"And I did not create the jinn and mankind except to worship Me."*
> (Qur'an, Adh-Dhāriyāt 51:56)

Creation serves two grand, interrelated purposes:

1. **The Manifestation of God's Names and Attributes**
2. The universe is a living reflection of God's qualities—His mercy in the rain, His wisdom in the balance of nature, His justice in consequence, and His power in the heavens and earth.
3. Through creation, His names are witnessed, experienced, and known. The world is not random; it is a divine signature in motion.
4. **The Moral Testing of Humanity**
5. Life is a field of moral responsibility where human beings are tested in their freedom, choices, and actions.
6. This testing distinguishes the sincere from the false, the upright from the corrupt, and allows reward and justice to be assigned with perfect equity.

Creation, then, is not absurd or meaningless. It is part of a coherent, purposeful system designed with divine knowledge, mercy, and justice.

Third: Continuous Creation and Divine Management

Creation was not a one-time event; it is an ongoing reality.

God not only originated the universe—He continuously manages and sustains it:

41

- He gives life and causes death.
- He provides sustenance and grants guidance.
- He elevates and abases, brings ease or hardship, and turns hearts according to His wisdom.

> *"He arranges [every] matter from the heaven to the earth."*
>   (Qur'an, As-Sajdah 32:5)

This divine management affirms that the universe is not abandoned after its creation.

Rather, it exists under the constant and direct care of the Lord—who governs all things in perfect knowledge and will.

Fourth: Creation as the Key to Understanding Life and Death

To understand human existence—birth, life, death, and beyond—we must first understand creation.

- **Birth** is not emergence from true nonexistence, but a transition from the unseen to the seen, from one phase of divine will to another.
- **Life** is not a meaningless episode; it is the **arena of the test**, where moral responsibility is enacted.
- **Death** is not the end of existence, but a **gateway** to the unseen realm: through the Barzakh (intermediate state), to resurrection, judgment, and eternal destiny.

Thus, belief in God as the Creator is not just a theological assertion—it is the **foundation** upon which the entire worldview of Islam rests.

It is what gives meaning to life, direction to our actions, and clarity to our ultimate end.

Conclusion

Creation is the first divine act that inaugurated the story of existence.

It is the doorway through which the human being begins to understand themselves, their Lord, and their purpose.

Whoever neglects the reality of creation walks in confusion—unsure of why they live, and unaware of where they are going.

But the one who knows the Creator—

who understands that all things begin with Him and return to Him—

walks the path of truth with clarity, humility, and purpose.

For they understand not only where they are,

but why they were brought into being—

and where their journey ultimately leads.

The Meaning of Creation

In the authentic Islamic worldview, the concept of creation carries a meaning far deeper than any superficial or materialistic interpretation.

Creation is the act of bringing something into existence from **absolute nothingness**—without prior model or material—by the will, knowledge, and power of the Creator.

This divine act is fundamentally distinct from anything human beings do:

- Humans fashion things from pre-existing materials.
- God, exalted is He, originated **matter, time, space, energy, and the laws that govern them**, without need, precedent, or assistance.

As the Qur'an affirms:

> *"The Originator of the heavens and the earth."*
> *(Qur'an, Al-Baqarah 2:117)*

—meaning He brought them into being with no prior example, through absolute power and perfect wisdom.

Creation Includes:

- **The initial origination** — the bringing into existence of the universe, life, humanity, and even death itself.
- **Ongoing sustenance** — the continual management, care, and gov-

ernance of all created things in accordance with their purpose and position.

Creation is not a one-time mechanical act that concluded at some distant point in the past. It is an ongoing expression of divine will—a relationship of **constant nurturing, sustenance, and governance** between the Creator and His creation.

> *"But they are in confusion over a new creation."*
> *(Qur'an, Qāf 50:15)*

Creation in the Qur'an

The Qur'an reveals key dimensions of the act of creation:

Exclusivity:

> *"Allah is the Creator of all things."*
> *(Qur'an, Az-Zumar 39:62)*

Only God creates in the true sense—without partner or intermediary.

Perfection:

> *"Who perfected everything which He created."*
> *(Qur'an, As-Sajdah 32:7)*

Creation reflects meticulous design and complete wisdom.

Purpose:

"Did you think that We created you aimlessly?"
(Qur'an, Al-Mu'minūn 23:115)

Creation is not random—it is purposeful, deliberate, and filled with moral and existential meaning.

The Philosophical Dimension of Creation

The reality of divine creation exposes the inadequacies of both absurdist thought and pure materialism:

- Nonexistence cannot give rise to existence.
- Lifeless matter cannot generate consciousness or intelligence.
- Complex, ordered systems cannot emerge from chaos without direction or will.

These principles—acknowledged by both Islamic theologians like **al-Ghazālī** and classical philosophers—affirm that **recognizing creation as a deliberate, wise act of a transcendent Creator** is the most coherent explanation for the existence of the universe, life, and the human soul.

This understanding also guards against the existential nihilism that often follows from denying creation—offering instead a vision of reality rooted in purpose, balance, and moral clarity.

Conclusion

In Islam, creation is:

- A **wise origination** from nothingness,
- Carried out with **intention and purpose**,

- Executed with **perfection and care**,
- By a **single Creator**, infinite in power and limitless in wisdom.

He who understands the meaning of creation grasps not only the secret of existence,

but also the dignity of human life, the purpose of every breath, and the direction of the soul's ultimate return.

To know the Creator is to know why we live,

and to understand creation is to begin the journey back to the One who made us.

The Philosophy of the Purpose of Creation

One of the most enduring and profound questions in both philosophy and faith is:

Why was the universe created? Why was humanity brought into existence?

The Islamic worldview, unlike many speculative philosophies, offers a clear and comprehensive answer—one that harmonizes revealed scripture with rational contemplation.

In Islam, creation is neither an act of absurdity nor the product of blind chance.

It is a purposeful, deliberate act, driven by divine wisdom, mercy, and justice—directed toward meaningful ends.

First: Manifestation of God's Names and Attributes

God, exalted is He, is absolutely perfect and self-sufficient. He has no need for creation out of deficiency or incompleteness.

Yet by His wisdom, He willed to manifest the beauty and perfection of His names and attributes through the created world:

- His name **Al-Khāliq (The Creator)** is expressed through the existence of all things.
- His mercy is revealed in the care and provision given to living beings.
- His justice is seen in the moral order of reward and punishment.
- His wisdom is evident in the fine-tuned balance of the cosmos and the guidance of revelation.

Thus, creation is a mirror reflecting the majesty of God's names and attributes—a canvas upon which His perfection is displayed for those who reflect.

While God remains utterly independent of His creation, the world becomes a means through which His beauty is known and His presence recognized.

Second: Testing and Trial of Humanity

From among all creation, the human being was granted a unique gift: **free will**, and with it, the responsibility of conscious servitude to God.

> *"And I did not create the jinn and mankind except to worship Me."*
> *(Qur'an, Adh-Dhāriyāt 51:56)*

This worship is not merely ritual, but a comprehensive submission to divine will—expressed through intention, action, and ethical conduct.

The world, then, is not a place of permanence, but a **domain of testing**:

- Will the human being embrace their higher calling and submit willingly to their Creator?
- Or will they turn away in arrogance, living as though life has no purpose?

The divine path (*Shariah*) provides the guidance by which one may pass this test—illuminating the way to truth, balance, and salvation.

Third: Stewardship and the Cultivation of the Earth

Humanity was not only created to worship, but also to serve as **God's stewards (khulafā') on earth**—entrusted with the moral and material development of the world.

> *"Indeed, I will make upon the earth a successive authority."*
> (Qur'an, Al-Baqarah 2:30)

This stewardship (*khilāfah*) is not a license for domination or exploitation, but a responsibility to manage creation in accordance with God's guidance:

- To establish justice and prevent corruption.
- To build societies grounded in truth, equity, and mercy.
- To pursue knowledge and advance civilization without severing it from spiritual and ethical roots.

This is the foundation of Islamic civilization: where technological progress and governance are measured by their alignment with divine values.

Fourth: Manifestation of Human Distinction and Moral Clarity

Creation also serves to unveil the moral reality of the human being:

- The **believer** ascends through knowledge of God, sincerity, and obedience.
- The **disbeliever** descends through denial, arrogance, and heedlessness.

This distinction is not arbitrary—it unfolds through human choice and is judged by God's perfect justice.

> *"So that he who perished [through disbelief] would perish upon evidence and he who lived [through faith] would live upon evidence."*
> *(Qur'an, Al-Anfāl 8:42)*

In this way, creation becomes the stage upon which truth is revealed and justice is fulfilled—both in this world and the next.

Conclusion

The purpose of creation in Islam rests upon four interwoven realities:

- The **manifestation of God's perfection and beauty** through His names and attributes.
- The **testing of humanity** through responsible moral freedom.
- The **cultivation and stewardship of the earth** as a trust and divine assignment.
- The **clarification of human ranks** through free will and accountability.

51

Through these dimensions, God's wisdom, justice, and mercy become manifest in the order of creation.

The human being is not left adrift in meaninglessness, but is guided along a clear path—

a journey of awareness, responsibility, and return.

Everything in creation is purposeful.

Every being has a role.

And humanity alone is entrusted to fulfill that role—

with reason, with heart, and with choice.

The Universe — The Open Signs of God

Introduction

In every atom of existence, in every orbiting planet, every drop of water, and every living cell,

a resounding truth emerges:

There exists a Creator—Great, Wise, Knowledgeable, and Powerful.

In the Islamic worldview, the universe is not a mute backdrop to human drama.

It is a living sign, an open book inscribed with the language of harmony, order, and meaning.

Its verses are not inked in script but woven into the fabric of existence—calling us to read with insight, not heedlessness.

As Allah says:

> *"We will show them Our signs in the horizons and within themselves until it becomes clear to them that it is the truth."*
> *(Qur'an, Fussilat 41:53)*

First: The Universe as Testimony to the Creator

The cosmos, in all its detail and magnitude, proclaims the handiwork of a deliberate Designer:

- From the precision of subatomic particles to the majesty of galactic formations,
- From the laws of physics to the patterns of life,
- Nothing operates without purpose or balance.

Every part of the universe—from the pulse of stars to the swirl of DNA—functions with precise calibration.

This coherence reveals not randomness, but rulership. Not chaos, but conscious command.

Each part of creation is a living witness, pointing to the oneness, perfection, and sovereignty of God.

Second: Order and Precision in Creation

The Qur'an consistently draws our attention to the exactness of the natural world:

- The succession of night and day
- The orbits of celestial bodies
- The interdependence of ecosystems
- The balance of elements sustaining life

Allah says:

> *"And the sun runs [its course] for a term [appointed]; that is the determination of the Exalted in Might, the Knowing."*
> *(Qur'an, Yā Sīn 36:38)*

Such intricate order cannot arise from blind chance.

It is the unmistakable trace of a Wise Creator, whose will governs both the macrocosm of galaxies and the microcosm of life.

Third: The Universe as an Open Sign for Humanity

God did not create the universe in vain.

He designed it as a **field of reflection**, inviting human beings to ponder, question, and awaken:

- Its signs call to the **fitrah** (natural disposition) within us.
- Its patterns stir the intellect and invite honest inquiry.
- Its beauty and balance resonate with the soul's yearning for truth.

As Allah declares:

> *"Indeed, in the creation of the heavens and the earth and the alternation of the night and the day are signs for those of understanding."*
> *(Qur'an, Āl 'Imrān 3:190)*

To reflect on creation is not just science—it is worship.

For those with open hearts and minds, the universe becomes a classroom of truth and a mirror to the Divine.

Fourth: The Universe as a Path to Deepened Faith and Spiritual Excellence (Ihsan)

Reflecting upon the universe is not a luxury; it is a path to **spiritual excellence**:

- It strengthens **faith** by reinforcing God's greatness and nearness.
- It nurtures **ihsan**—to worship God as though you see Him.
- It cultivates humility, gratitude, and awe.

Scientific knowledge, when joined with spiritual insight, becomes an act of devotion.

To understand the cosmos with reverence is to stand in awe of the One who created it.

Every reflection on the stars, the sea, or the soul is an opportunity to remember God, glorify Him, and walk the earth with greater mindfulness.

Fifth: The Universe is a Means, Not an End

In Islam, the universe is a **created, subjugated reality**, not an independent source of power or meaning:

- Its beauty is a sign, not the object of worship.
- Its precision calls us to trust in divine wisdom, not to idolize material laws.
- Its vastness humbles us and reminds us of the One who is beyond it all.

The purpose of reflecting on the universe is not to lose ourselves in its wonder,

but to be led through it—to the Creator who shaped it with care and purpose.

The universe is the path, not the destination.

Conclusion

In the Islamic worldview, the universe is a grand revelation—
a perpetual signbook written not with words, but with existence.

- To reflect on it is to witness God's oneness.
- To ignore it is to lose the keys to meaning.

Let us read the universe with **awakened hearts** and **conscious minds**—
And let every gust of wind, every shining star, and every blooming flower
become a mirror in which we behold the signs of the One who created
all things in truth.

Order and Precision in the Universe

Among the clearest rational and intuitive signs pointing to the existence of God and the perfection of His wisdom is the astonishing order and precise design that permeate the universe.

The cosmos is not a chaotic, meaningless expanse.

Rather, it is a finely tuned system—regulated by consistent laws, coordinated interactions, and harmonious relationships at every scale of existence.

First: Features of Cosmic Order

The evidence for this design appears in countless facets of the universe. Consider just a few:

1. Coordination Among Celestial Bodies

- The motion of stars and planets follows precise gravitational laws.
- The alternation of night and day occurs due to the Earth's rotation and its orbital path around the sun.
- The four seasons result from the Earth's axial tilt—finely calibrated to sustain life and ecological balance.

2. Stability of Natural Laws

- Physical constants—like gravity and electromagnetism—operate with astonishing consistency across the universe.
- Chemical and biological laws govern matter and life, from atomic interactions to the structure of DNA, in ways that are stable, testable, and universal.

3. Delicate Balance for Life on Earth

- The Earth's atmosphere contains precise proportions of gases vital for life.
- The water and carbon cycles maintain environmental stability and support all ecosystems.
- Biodiversity exists within a fragile balance that, if disrupted slightly, would lead to collapse.

4. Intricate Design in Living Organisms

- The living cell, the basic unit of life, operates as a miniature factory—guided by DNA, a molecular language that governs development, function, and inheritance.
- The nervous system, circulatory system, and even the human eye reveal an interdependent complexity that defies reduction to mere accident.

Second: The Implications of This Order and Precision

The sheer regularity and complexity of the universe demand deeper reflection. These features are not incidental—they are signposts pointing to something beyond the material.

1. Order Exceeds What Chance Alone Can Explain

The high degree of coordination seen in physical laws, biological systems, and cosmic mechanics makes it implausible to attribute everything to random chance.

While elements of unpredictability exist within nature, the overarching structure and consistency defy the logic of pure accident.

2. Necessity of a Conscious Designer

Systems that exhibit interdependent, goal-directed function—especially at multiple levels—logically imply the work of an intentional, knowledgeable mind.

Design, when observed in any other context, always points back to intelligence.

3. Evidence of Purpose and Wisdom

This precision is not without direction. The universe operates toward specific ends: sustaining life, maintaining balance, producing beauty and energy.

Such purposeful orientation affirms that creation is guided—not random, but ruled by the will of a Wise Creator.

Third: The Qur'an and the Harmony of Creation

The Qur'an frequently calls attention to the order of the cosmos as evidence of God's existence, unity, and perfection:

> "The handiwork of Allah, who perfected all things."
> (Qur'an, An-Naml 27:88)

"Who created and proportioned."
  (Qur'an, Al-A'lā 87:2)

Through these verses, the Qur'an reminds us that:

- Creation is **balanced** and measured.
- Every component has been **proportioned** to fulfill its role.
- The parts of creation are **interconnected**, working together to reflect divine purpose.

Thus, reflecting on the cosmos is not only an intellectual exercise—it is a spiritual path.

Contemplation of the universe leads the sincere soul to the recognition of the Creator.

Conclusion

The harmony, stability, and interwoven design of the universe are not random curiosities.

They are signs—messages embedded in creation—inviting every reflective mind and open heart to recognize the One behind it all.

As human understanding deepens through science and observation,

so too does the certainty grow that this miraculous system could not have emerged without will, knowledge, and power.

It is the signature of the All-Wise, the All-Powerful—the One who brought all things into being with order, beauty, and purpose.

The Universe as a Stage for Testing

In the comprehensive Islamic worldview, the universe is not a purposeless expanse of matter, nor a field of random events devoid of value.

Rather, it is a **vast, intentional stage**—carefully prepared by the Creator to serve as the arena for the **testing of human beings**, testing their choices, responsibilities, and moral worth.

First: The Cosmic Stage Prepared for Testing

God created the universe with precision, not only to sustain life, but to provide the perfect conditions for the human moral trial:

- The Earth is finely tuned for habitation—with atmosphere, water, vegetation, mountains, and ecological balance, all perfectly calibrated.
- The human soul is equipped with the capacity to choose—between good and evil, faith and denial, sincerity and arrogance.
- The intellect is endowed with the faculties of thought, reasoning, and discernment—enabling reflection, moral judgment, and understanding.

> *"Indeed, We created man from a sperm-drop mixture that We may try him."*
> *(Qur'an, Al-Insān 76:2)*

This divine trial (*ibtilā'*) is not a punishment—it is a process of refinement, an unveiling of one's truth, and a test of one's readiness for their eternal destiny.

Second: Humanity as the Center of the Test

With the universe thus prepared, the human being is placed at its moral center.

The Earth and all that it contains—its lands, oceans, seasons, and resources—have been subjugated not for vanity, but for responsibility:

- Will the human being use these gifts with gratitude or ingratitude?
- Will they build with justice or corrupt through arrogance?
- Will they recognize the Giver, or become lost in the gift?

> *"It is He who made the earth tame for you—so walk among its slopes and eat of His provision—and to Him is the resurrection."*
> *(Qur'an, Al-Mulk 67:15)*

Thus, the universe is not an end in itself, but a **means**—a support system for the human journey toward conscious servitude, accountability, and return to God.

Third: The Signs of the Universe and Their Role in the Test

The universe is not silent. It speaks—through signs that appeal to both the intellect and the soul:

- The alternation of night and day reflects divine precision.
- The diversity of languages and colors points to intentionality and richness in design.
- The emergence, order, and interdependence of life reveal profound

wisdom and power.

> *"And on the earth are signs for the certain [in faith] * and in yourselves.*
> *Then will you not see?"*
> (Qur'an, Adh-Dhāriyāt 51:20–21)

The test lies in whether one reflects or ignores:

- The one who observes, ponders, and humbles himself increases in clarity and faith.
- The one who turns away in arrogance closes the very window through which truth is seen.

Fourth: The Universe as a Field of Freedom and Accountability

Freedom is not merely permitted—it is **granted** by God as a core element of the test:

- Each person chooses their path, exercising moral will within the framework of divine and natural laws.
- Actions are weighed, and consequences follow.

Here, divine justice is manifest in its fullness:

- None is rewarded without merit.
- None is punished without knowledge or evidence.
- Every soul reaps the harvest of its own sowing.

This justice is rooted in complete knowledge, perfect wisdom, and full accountability—nothing is hidden from the One who sees all.

Conclusion

The universe is the grand stage upon which the human journey unfolds:

- A stage richly endowed with signs, provisions, and guidance.
- A stage where moral freedom is honored, and moral accountability assured.
- A stage that culminates in resurrection, reckoning, and reward or loss.

Whoever reads this universe with **mind and heart** will discover the path that leads to their Creator—clear, compelling, and filled with light.

But whoever closes their eyes to its signs,

and hardens their heart against its meaning,

will wander through life unanchored—only to awaken to the truth when it is too late.

So walk the stage with awareness. Choose with sincerity. And know that the One who prepared it watches, guides, and waits.

III

The Human Being, Birth, and Life — The Project of Existence

The human being stands at the heart of the project of existence—as the bearer of a divine trust, uniquely composed of both body and soul, and fully responsible for their choices. Birth marks the beginning of this profound journey, filled with existential meaning and divine intention. Life, in this framework, is not a random occurrence but an abode of trial, a purposeful test in which the individual is called to strive, race toward good deeds, and fulfill their role as a servant of God with awareness, responsibility, and sincerity.

Awakening to Responsibility and the Eternal Journey

Introduction

Having explored God the Creator, the first act of creation, and the universe as a field of divine trial,

we now arrive at the most responsible participant in this grand design:

The Human Being.

In the Islamic worldview, the human being is not a peripheral spectator in the theater of existence,

but its central actor—**the bearer of the Supreme Trust** (*al-amānah*) that the heavens, the earth, and the mountains declined to carry.

All that is in the universe has been **subjugated for him,**

All that is in divine revelation is **directed to him,**

And all that pertains to life and the Hereafter is **shaped by his choices and actions**.

This part of our journey brings us face to face with the foundational existential questions:

- Who is the human being, in origin and essence? What defines his true nature?

- What does birth truly signify? Is it merely biological entry, or the beginning of an eternal journey?
- How should life be understood? What purpose does it serve, and how should one live it?
- How must one approach life—as a trial to navigate, not merely a pleasure to consume?

First: The Human Being — Honored and Responsible

We will uncover how the human being is a remarkable synthesis:

- Body and soul,
- Instinct and intellect,
- Freedom and accountability.

He was uniquely prepared to carry the trust that all of creation declined—a role that requires both humility and nobility.

Second: Birth — The Launch of the Eternal Project

Birth is not a mere biological event.
It is a divine declaration—the beginning of **moral responsibility**,
a transition into the realm of trial and consequence,
the starting point of an ascent—or descent—toward eternal destiny.

Third: Life — The Arena of Action and Fulfillment

Life is not a playground for whims or a marketplace of distraction.
It is the **arena for moral effort**, a **test of conscience**, and the **domain of conscious servitude**.

- Life is short—but it is decisive.
- It is charged with choices that shape one's eternal standing.

- Every moment matters; every act echoes beyond this world.

The Centrality of This Part

The human being is the **link between creation and purpose**.
Birth marks the entrance into moral accountability.
Life is the ground on which eternal destiny is written.
To understand this triad—the human being, birth, and life—is to gain clarity on everything else:
On the self, on God, on the universe, and on the Hereafter.

A Call to Begin

Here begins the greatest existential journey of all:

- To uncover the reality of who we are.
- To understand why we were created.
- To make the most of this fleeting life in pursuit of eternal nearness to the Creator.

Let our minds be ready to reflect,
our hearts open to receive,
and our will firm enough to walk the path with purpose.

> *"He has succeeded who purifies it, and he has failed who corrupts it."*
> *(Qur'an, Ash-Shams 91:9–10)*

71

The Human Being — The Bearer of the Trust

Introduction

Having introduced the human being as the central figure in the universe and the recipient of divine purpose,

we now arrive at his most defining distinction:

He is the bearer of the Supreme Trust (*al-amānah*).

Among all the countless creatures that populate the universe,

it is the human being who holds a unique position and an extraordinary responsibility.

As Allah says:

> *"Indeed, We offered the Trust to the heavens and the earth and the mountains, but they declined to bear it and feared it; but man undertook to bear it. Indeed, he was unjust and ignorant."*
> *(Qur'an, Al-Aḥzāb 33:72)*

What is this *trust*?

Why did only the human accept it?

And what does it mean for his place in creation?

First: The Nature of the Trust

In the Qur'anic context, the *amānah* (trust) refers to the full weight of conscious moral responsibility:

- The duty to worship God voluntarily, without coercion.
- The freedom to choose between obedience and disobedience.
- The acceptance of divine revelation as guidance, embraced by reason and will.

Unlike angels, who obey by nature, and inanimate creation, which follows divine decree unconsciously,
the human being was created with **intellect, free will**, and **moral agency**.
He alone carries the burden and honor of choosing his path—with eternal consequences.

Second: The Dual Composition of the Human Being

To fulfill this sacred trust, the human being was crafted as a **synthesis of dualities**:

- **Body and Soul** — a physical vessel of clay, and a soul breathed from the command of God.
- **Reason and Desire** — the capacity to reflect and restrain, alongside instinctual impulses.
- **Freedom and Accountability** — autonomy in choice, yet answerable for every deed.

This complex nature positions the human being uniquely:
He can **rise to angelic heights** through submission and virtue,
or **fall to animalistic depths** through heedlessness and defiance.

Third: The Human Being's Rank Among Creation

By accepting the trust, the human being was granted a station of profound honor:

- Created by God's own hand and infused with His spirit.
- Welcomed to existence with the prostration of the angels to Adam.
- Appointed as **khalīfah** (steward) on Earth—to cultivate it in alignment with divine justice.

As Allah says:

> *"And We have certainly honored the children of Adam."*
> *(Qur'an, Al-Isrā' 17:70)*

But this honor is not unconditional.
It is tied to the fulfillment of the trust:

- He who fulfills it is elevated and draws near to God.
- He who neglects it dishonors his soul and descends to ruin.

Fourth: The Implications of Carrying the Trust

The trust is not symbolic—it demands a lifelong commitment:

1. **Belief in God and His Revelation** — affirming truth and submitting to guidance.
2. **Righteous Action** — living in servitude through everyday deeds.
3. **Moral Awareness** — recognizing that every word and action is subject to divine judgment.
4. **Spiritual and Social Reform** — striving to purify the soul, resist injustice, and uphold truth.

Thus, the human being does not live in vain.

He carries a grand cosmic mission—accountable before God,
before the world he influences,
and before his own conscience.

Fifth: The Danger of Betraying the Trust

To betray the trust is to:

- Live in heedlessness of divine purpose.
- Deviate from the path of *fitrah* and rational clarity.
- Invite divine justice, which is never without proof or mercy.

The weight of the trust is immense:

- Its **honor** is the highest.
- Its **responsibility** is grave.
- Its **outcome** is decisive: either eternal reward in Paradise or rightful punishment in Hell.

Conclusion

In the Islamic perspective, the human being is not a creature adrift in chance,

nor driven purely by base instinct.
He is a **moral agent, a conscious soul,**
the bearer of a trust accepted by his own free will—
placed upon the earth to be tested in fulfilling it.

> *"He has succeeded who purifies it, and he has failed who corrupts it."*
> *(Qur'an, Ash-Shams 91:9–10)*

To remember the trust is to live with purpose and dignity.

To forget it is to lose the self—both in this world and in the world to come.

The Physical and Spiritual Composition of the Human Being

Introduction

In the Islamic worldview, the human being is a uniquely crafted creation—
not merely a body of flesh, nor a spirit adrift, but a **synthesis of two distinct realms**:

- **Matter**, which anchors him to the earth,
- **Spirit**, which elevates him toward the unseen world.

This dual composition gives the human being his **dignity, complexity**, and **responsibility**— explaining his inner tensions, elevated potential, and central role in the divine test of life.

First: The Material Element — A Body from Clay

The human's physical origin is rooted in the earth.

> *"He created him from dust."*
> *(Qur'an, Āl 'Imrān 3:59)*

"And We did certainly create man from an extract of clay."
    (Qur'an, Al-Mu'minūn 23:12)

- The human body is composed of elemental substances—water, minerals, and organic compounds.
- It is nourished by earthly food and interacts with the material world through sensation and action.
- It experiences desires, fatigue, pleasure, and decay—reminding us of our earthly origin.

This bodily nature enables interaction with the world and grounds the human in a **physiological and instinctual reality**.

Second: The Spiritual Element — A Breath from God's Command

Alongside his material form, the human was given a soul—a divine infusion that transcends the physical.

"And when I have fashioned him and breathed into him of My spirit..."
    (Qur'an, Ṣād 38:72)

- The spirit is not derived from matter—it is a command from God, unseen and elevated.
- It is the source of **consciousness, moral intuition, spiritual longing, and accountability**.
- It grants the human the capacity for **worship, knowledge, self-awareness, and the pursuit of higher meaning**.

Through the spirit, the human is drawn toward transcendence—seeking

God, purpose, and eternal truth.

Third: The Integration of Matter and Spirit

These two dimensions—**body and spirit**—are not in conflict, but in **constant interaction**.

- The body serves as the vessel through which the spirit acts in the world.
- The spirit directs the body toward virtue, meaning, and self-restraint.

When the two are held in harmony:

- The human being lives with dignity, purpose, and balance.
- If the body dominates and the spirit is neglected, man descends into **heedlessness and excess**.
- If spirituality is pursued in isolation from the body's reality, life becomes **disconnected and dysfunctional**.

Islam calls for a **balanced integration**—not extreme asceticism, and not material indulgence:

- Not an escape from the world,
- Nor immersion in it without soul.

Rather, a **middle path** where both realms are honored and guided by revelation.

Fourth: The Responsibilities of Dual Composition

Because the human being is composed of both body and spirit, he is entrusted with a twofold responsibility:

- **The rights of the body**—maintaining its health, cleanliness, and lawful

nourishment.
- **The rights of the spirit**—purifying the soul, engaging in worship, and striving for moral elevation.

Life, then, becomes a **holistic project**:
to nurture both elements in harmony, so that the human may fulfill his **ultimate purpose**—
Servitude to God through free will, conscious understanding, and balanced living.

Conclusion

The human being is not simply a lump of clay, nor a disembodied spirit.
He is a **divine synthesis**:

- **Formed from earth,**
- **Animated by spirit,**
- **Guided by reason,**
- **Tested through freedom,**
- **Called to walk between earth and heaven.**

> *"And [He] proportioned him and breathed into him of His spirit."*
> *(Qur'an, As-Sajdah 32:9)*

Whoever understands this composition understands his function.
And whoever neglects either part—body or spirit—loses balance, loses meaning, and ultimately loses himself.

Human Responsibility for His Choices

Introduction

One of the essential consequences of the human being's intellectual and spiritual composition is that he is a **creature of moral agency—**

endowed with **free will**, capable of choosing between alternatives, and bearing full responsibility for his decisions.

In the Islamic worldview, this freedom is not absolute chaos or blind autonomy.

It is **a trust**, regulated by divine wisdom, and linked to the great truths that define human existence and ultimate destiny.

First: The Freedom to Choose

God granted the human being genuine moral freedom—freedom within the scope of responsibility:

- He may choose faith or denial, righteousness or sin, reform or corruption.
- This capacity is what dignifies the human being and qualifies him for divine testing.

> *"So whoever wills—let him believe; and whoever wills—let him disbelieve."*
>   (Qur'an, Al-Kahf 18:29)

This freedom is what makes praise, blame, reward, and punishment meaningful:

- If human beings were forced, **divine justice would be obscured**.
- If they were left without guidance, **the purpose of creation would be nullified**.

Freedom is not simply the ability to choose; it is the ability to choose **with awareness and accountability**.

Second: The Boundaries of Freedom

But this freedom is not limitless.

- It is **constrained by human capacity**—one cannot will beyond their means.
- It is **bounded by physical laws** and the natural order established by God.
- And it is **subject to the overarching divine will**, which encompasses all things.

Yet within the realm of moral responsibility—belief, worship, justice, and conduct—
   the human being possesses **real choice**. It is this moral zone where divine testing takes place.
   Freedom, then, is not the absence of all constraint—it is the meaningful opportunity to choose between right and wrong under God's gaze.

Third: Full Responsibility for One's Choices

Because the human being is free, he is accountable.

He bears the weight of his every intention, word, and action:

- What he chooses to pursue.
- What he avoids or neglects.
- What he conceals within and expresses outwardly.

He will stand before God's perfect justice—where **no soul is wronged**, and every deed is revealed.

> "And the record [of deeds] will be placed [open], and you will see the criminals fearful of what is [recorded] therein."
> (Qur'an, Al-Kahf 18:49)

Islam teaches that **intention** (*niyyah*) holds profound weight:

- A small deed with pure intention can outweigh a large act done in vanity.
- Even silent inner choices are recorded, for God knows what is in every heart.

Thus, **responsibility in Islam begins not with action, but with consciousness**.

Fourth: Choice and Eternal Destiny

The choices a human being makes in this life **construct the path to his afterlife**:

- Whoever chooses faith, humility, and righteousness walks toward Paradise and God's pleasure.

- Whoever chooses arrogance, disbelief, and corruption heads toward regret and punishment.

Every moment of life contains a decision—spoken or unspoken—that shapes eternity:

- A word of truth or a word of harm.
- A step toward light or a step into heedlessness.

"So whoever does an atom's weight of good will see it,
and whoever does an atom's weight of evil will see it."
(Qur'an, Az-Zalzalah 99:7–8)

Conclusion

The human being is entrusted with freedom not as a burden, but as a divine honor:

- His **freedom is a trust** granted by God.
- His **choices are a testimony** written by his own hand.
- His **destiny is the natural fruit of what he chose to pursue, love, and live for.**

Whoever lives with awareness of this responsibility moves with sincerity toward his Lord.

And whoever is heedless of it drifts from the path—losing not only his worldly purpose but his eternal home.

Birth — The Beginning of the Story

Introduction

Though often seen as a mere biological milestone,
in the comprehensive Islamic worldview, **birth is far more than a physical transition** from the womb to the world.
It marks the **beginning of a profound existential journey—**
the opening scene of a story that stretches from earthly life, through the Barzakh, and into eternal permanence.
In this view, birth is not incidental. It is:

- A **declaration of entry** into the realm of trial,
- The **initiation of moral preparation,**
- And the moment the human being receives the **trust (amānah)** he accepted before time.

First: Birth as Entry into the Realm of Trial

> *"[He] who created death and life to test you [as to] which of you is best in deed."*
> *(Qur'an, Al-Mulk 67:2)*

With birth begins the stage of worldly life:

- The domain of testing,
- Where belief and behavior are tried,
- And where intention and will gradually awaken to purpose.

Though the newborn is not yet morally accountable,
   he is a **soul in formation**, destined to one day choose between guidance and misguidance, faith and denial.

Second: The Features of Human Existence at Birth

From the moment of birth, the human being begins progressing through defined stages:

- From weakness to strength,
- From ignorance to understanding,
- From dependence to agency.

> *"It is Allah who created you from weakness, then made after weakness strength, then made after strength weakness and gray hair."*
>   *(Qur'an, Al-Rūm 30:54)*

The newborn is not a blank slate, but is **divinely equipped**:

- With the **innate disposition (fitrah)** inclined toward tawḥīd,
- The **potential for intellect, learning, and moral growth,**
- And the **instincts of survival and curiosity** needed for development.

These gifts prepare him to one day bear the burden of responsibility with awareness and choice.

Third: The Responsibility of Upbringing After Birth

Birth alone does not complete the human being.

It must be followed by **nurturing that honors the dual nature** of man—body and soul.

The Prophet ﷺ said:

> "Every child is born upon the natural disposition (fitrah), but it is his parents who make him a Jew, a Christian, or a Magian."
> (Narrated by al-Bukhārī and Muslim)

This ḥadīth reminds us that **environment and education shape the soul**—either guiding it or distorting its nature.

Thus, the early years become a **crucial phase of cultivation**:

- Building faith,
- Developing character,
- And forming a consciousness of life's greater purpose.

Fourth: Birth as the Beginning of Eternal Destiny

From the instant of birth, a human being enters a **cosmic equation**:

- A soul tested through time,
- A life racing toward judgment,
- A heart writing its future with every passing day.

Though **moral accountability begins at maturity**,

the journey of **moral formation and spiritual preparation** begins at birth.

Each stage of life is a step forward—or backward—on the road to:

- Eternal joy,

- Or everlasting regret.

> *"So whoever does an atom's weight of good will see it,*
> *and whoever does an atom's weight of evil will see it."*
> *(Qur'an, Az-Zalzalah 99:7–8)*

Fifth: Birth and Human Dignity

In Islam, every human being is **born with dignity**—not as a random product of biology,
   but as a creation honored from the very beginning.

> *"And We have certainly honored the children of Adam."*
> *(Qur'an, Al-Isrā' 17:70)*

This dignity entails more than status:

- It is a **right to life,**
- A **right to be nurtured,**
- A **right to seek knowledge,**
- A **right to be guided to truth.**

It is also a **call to moral responsibility**:
   To live with purpose, freedom, and a consciousness of one's noble origin and destined return.

Conclusion

Birth, in the Islamic worldview, is not merely a beginning.
   It is the **start of a sacred narrative**:

- A story of a soul entrusted with divine responsibility,
- A being called to choose between light and darkness,
- A life shaped by decision and destined for eternal consequence.

To grasp the meaning of birth is to **grasp the purpose of life—**
and to begin walking the path that prepares for what lies beyond.

The Existential Meaning of Birth

Introduction

In the comprehensive Islamic worldview, **birth is far more than a biological event** recorded in the timeline of physical existence.

It is not simply the body's entry into the world, but the **unfolding of a divine trust**,

a signal that the human being has entered the realm of conscious trial and moral purpose.

It marks the beginning of a sacred journey—

a return to a responsibility once accepted in the unseen realm, now lived out in time, choice, and consequence.

This chapter explores how birth, in Islam, is not a beginning from nothing, but the **awakening of a mission**, a trial, and a path to eternity.

First: Birth as a Declaration of Bearing the Trust

At the moment of birth, the human being enters the world as a bearer of the **divine trust (amānah)**—

a covenant made before creation, now ready to unfold through will, awareness, and action.

"And [mention] when your Lord took from the children of Adam—from their loins—their descendants and made them testify of themselves, [saying to them], 'Am I not your Lord?' They said, 'Yes, we have testified.'"

(*Qur'an, Al-A'rāf 7:172*)

Thus, birth does not mark the beginning of a new relationship with God,

but the **commencement of actualizing an ancient covenant**—through choices that reflect or betray that testimony.

Second: Birth as the Beginning of Responsibility and the Path to Completion

At birth, the human being is weak and unaware,

but divinely equipped with fitrah, potential, and the seeds of conscience.

- He progresses through stages of growth—physical, intellectual, and moral.
- His capacities expand until, at maturity, he becomes **fully accountable** before God.

While moral responsibility begins at maturity,

the journey toward that accountability—through development, learning, and moral exposure—begins at birth.

Thus, the human being is not immediately judged,

but is gradually prepared to bear the consequences of his freely made decisions.

Third: Birth as Entry into the Test of Time

From the first breath, time becomes both a gift and a test.

- The test of comfort and hardship,
- The test of health and illness,
- The test of knowledge and ignorance,
- The test of joy, fear, and moral decision.

These shifting states are not random.

They are **calibrated by divine wisdom** to expose the inner truth of each soul.

With every moment, the human being draws nearer to his final meeting with God—

whether he is conscious of it or not.

Fourth: Birth as a Reminder of Life's Impermanence

Because the human is born in weakness,

and because his condition constantly changes with age and circumstance,

his very existence **testifies to the reality of mortality**.

Though birth is a beginning,

it is also the **first step toward an inevitable end**.

> *"Everyone upon the earth will perish."*
> *(Qur'an, Ar-Raḥmān 55:26)*

The wise are those who, remembering the reality of death,

live this life not as a permanent residence—but as a passage.

Fifth: The Dignity and Sacredness of Birth

In Islam, birth is not a coincidence of biology.
  It is a moment of **divine honor and sacred potential**.

- The newborn is honored with rights—from the right to life and care, to the right to be guided.
- Islamic rites such as the **adhān**, ʿaqīqah, and **naming** express that birth is both a spiritual and social event.

> *"And We have certainly honored the children of Adam."*
>   *(Qur'an, Al-Isrāʾ 17:70)*

That dignity is not passive.
  It calls the human being to **freedom, responsibility, and spiritual stewardship**—to walk the earth with purpose.

Conclusion

In the Islamic conception, **birth is the awakening of the soul's journey in the visible world**:

- It is the unfolding of a sacred trust.
- The beginning of a life shaped by freedom, choice, and trial.
- The first step toward eternal reward—or loss.

Whoever fails to grasp the meaning of his beginning
  will fail to understand the meaning of his life—
  and will be unprepared for his return.

"Indeed we belong to Allah, and indeed to Him we will return."
(Qur'an, Al-Baqarah 2:156)

The Underlying Intention Behind Life

Introduction

In the Islamic worldview, human life is not a random movement or an aimless journey.

It is a **deliberate existential path**, shaped by divine wisdom and driven by an intention embedded in the very act of creation.

Behind every visible stage of life—birth, growth, success, struggle, and death—

lies a deeper reality: **a divine intention**, one that transcends survival, reproduction, and the pursuit of worldly pleasure.

The human being is called not only to recognize this intention but to **live by it**,

renewing it with every step in life's journey.

First: The Divine Intention in Creating Life

God did not create life playfully or without purpose.

> *"Does man think that he will be left neglected?"*
> *(Qur'an, Al-Qiyāmah 75:36)*

> *"Did you think that We created you aimlessly and that you would not be returned to Us?"*
> *(Qur'an, Al-Mu'minūn 23:115)*

The purpose behind life and creation is clear:

- To realize **voluntary servitude** (*'ubūdiyyah*) to God,
- To establish **truth, justice, and moral order** on Earth,
- And to test human beings—so that **deeds and intentions** may be rewarded with justice and mercy.

Thus, **divine intention is the source of life's meaning**—without it, life collapses into emptiness.

Second: The Human Intention Required for Life

As God created life with intention, the human being must live it with **intention aligned to that divine aim**.

This conscious intention entails:

- **Living for God and by God**—orienting all of life toward His worship and pleasure,
- **Viewing the world as a means, not an end**—a bridge to the Hereafter, not a final destination,
- **Pursuing the higher objectives of the Shariah (maqāṣid)**—which protect and promote religion, life, intellect, progeny, wealth, homeland, and the community.

These maqāṣid are not abstract ideals—they are the **ethical and social fruits of divine guidance**, shaping a life that is both **spiritually fulfilling** and **civically responsible**.

Life, then, is not the goal.

It is the **testbed of loyalty**, the arena in which the divine trust is carried or abandoned.

Third: The Impact of Intention in Guiding Life

Intention is the compass of the soul. It gives shape to all action, and weight to all deeds.

- It defines whether life is a **meaningless cycle** or a form of **continuous worship**.
- It determines the value of deeds—*even the simplest act may be elevated by a sincere intention.*
- It grants moral character to life—**the believer lives to reform the self and serve others**, not merely to indulge.

The Prophet ﷺ said:

> "Actions are judged by intentions, and each person will have what they intended."
> (Agreed upon)

Thus, intention becomes the **engine of purpose** behind:

- Physical behavior,
- Emotional motives,
- And intellectual pursuits.

Fourth: Renewing Intention Throughout the Journey of Life

Because life is constantly shifting—through tests, blessings, distractions, and doubts—

intention must be **regularly reviewed and renewed**.

- To realign when one's purpose strays,
- To recover clarity in times of heedlessness,
- To reconnect even mundane acts to the ultimate goal: **God's nearness and pleasure**.

Ibn al-Qayyim رحمه الله said:

"Intention is the soul of action, its guide and its driver; the action follows it."

A life of sincerity is not one of **perfect constancy**,

but of **continuous reorientation toward the One who never changes**.

Conclusion

The intention behind life is what separates:

- **A life of distraction, indulgence, and eventual regret,**

from

- **A life of clarity, direction, and eternal joy**.

He who lives without a higher intention will drift through days—busy, but empty.

But he who lives with **conscious purpose** will turn every breath into an act of worship,

and every moment into a step toward the Divine.

*"Indeed, those who say, 'Our Lord is Allah' and then remain steadfast—
angels descend upon them [saying], 'Do not fear or grieve but receive
glad tidings of Paradise, which you were promised.'"*
    (Qur'an, Fuṣṣilat 41:30)

Life — The Abode of Trial

Introduction

Once the human being begins his journey through birth,
  he enters a world of struggle, choice, and meaning: the domain of life.
  But in the Islamic worldview, life is not a chaotic playground nor a fleeting dream of pleasure.
  It is a **field of divine testing**—a purposeful arena where hearts, minds, and wills are refined.
  It is here, through deeds and decisions, that one's eternal destiny is shaped.

> *"And We test you with evil and with good as a trial."*
>   *(Qur'an, Al-Anbiyā' 21:35)*

First: The Nature of Worldly Life

Revelation describes this life with attributes that define its role as a trial:

- **Rapid Transience** — However long it seems, it is brief compared to the eternity that follows.
- **Constant Change** — Life fluctuates between wealth and poverty, strength and weakness, joy and fear.
- **Woven Contrasts** — Moments of laughter and grief, ease and hardship,

gain and loss, all coexist in one experience.

> *"This worldly life is but enjoyment [of delusion]."*
> (Qur'an, Āl 'Imrān 3:185)

Thus, life is not the destination. It is a **transit station**—to be crossed with clarity and caution.

Second: The Types of Trials in Life

Life's trials take many forms, each tailored to reveal what lies within us:

- **Blessings** — such as health, wealth, and influence, to test gratitude and uprightness.
- **Hardships** — like poverty, illness, and grief, to test patience and inner strength.
- **Desires and doubts** — subtle internal challenges to test sincerity and discipline.

> *"And We will surely test you with something of fear and hunger and a loss of wealth and lives and fruits..."*
> (Qur'an, Al-Baqarah 2:155)

No one escapes these trials—regardless of age, status, or condition.
Every soul is enrolled in the curriculum of testing.

Third: The Wisdom Behind Trial

These trials are not senseless. They are filled with divine wisdom:

- They **expose the depth of faith**—for true belief surfaces most clearly

under pressure.
- They **train the soul** in patience, gratitude, and reliance.
- They **purify and elevate**, expiating sins and refining character.
- They fulfill the demands of **divine justice**, ensuring that reward and punishment align with each person's response.

The world is the crucible in which sincerity is separated from show, and faith is forged through fire.

Fourth: Human Responses to Trial

In the face of trial, people respond in different ways:

- The **patient and grateful** rise in the ranks of the righteous.
- The **resentful and bitter** turn away, questioning divine decree and falling into darkness.
- The **heedless and distracted** waste their days in indulgence, unaware that time is slipping away.

Thus, **knowing the nature of trial** is among the believer's greatest tools for navigating life wisely.

Fifth: Making the Most of Life to Succeed in Trial

Since life is the arena of trial, the wise treat it as a **precious opportunity**:

- By hastening to do good,
- Living with mindfulness and purpose,
- Correcting intentions and returning often to repentance,
- And striving to serve God with excellence.

> *"And race toward forgiveness from your Lord and a Paradise as wide as the heavens and the earth."*
>   *(Qur'an, Āl 'Imrān 3:133)*

To those who see with insight, **the shortness of life becomes a ladder to eternity**.

Conclusion

This life is not the place of ultimate reward—
   it is the testing ground, the field of effort, the proving ground of faith.

- Whoever grasps its reality faces its trials with resolve—and transforms hardship into a path to eternal joy.
- But whoever is blinded by its illusions becomes enslaved to whims, losing both this world and the next.

So let us view life as the Creator intended:
   A field of struggle,
   A mirror of sincerity,
   And a path—if walked with faith—that ascends toward the pleasure of God.

Life as an Existential Test

Introduction

In the Islamic worldview, life is not a random biological episode or a social cycle without meaning.

It is a **profound moral and spiritual test**, designed to examine the human being at the deepest levels of his existence:

- In his **faith**,
- In his **reason**,
- In his **character**,
- And in his **will**.

> "That He may test you as to which of you is best in deed."
> (Qur'an, Hūd 11:7)

1. Life as a Field of Moral Exposure

Existential testing means that the human being is placed on this earth not to seek mere survival or pleasure,
but to walk a path where his **true self is revealed**—before himself, before others, and before God.

- Will he cling to truth or surrender to falsehood?
- Will his life reflect heedlessness or remembrance?

All aspects of existence—ease and hardship, light and darkness—are meticulously arranged to reveal the human being's response.

2. The Domains of Life's Test

This test unfolds in every dimension of daily life:

- **Belief** – Does he affirm God's oneness or chase his own desires?
- **Intention** – Does he seek God's pleasure or worldly praise?
- **Conduct** – Does he live with honesty and compassion, or with injustice and arrogance?
- **Blessings** – Does he express gratitude or become entitled?
- **Hardships** – Does he meet difficulty with patience or fall into despair?

Each day is a **new page in the divine examination**, and every decision a mark upon it.

3. A Test Founded on Justice and Truth

This test is neither arbitrary nor unjust. It is rooted in wisdom:

- It is **true**, because the human being is equipped with intellect, innate moral awareness (*fiṭrah*), and the freedom to choose.
- It is **just**, because the outcomes of Paradise or Hell are based on conscious choice, not compulsion.

> *"So that those who perished [through disbelief] would perish upon evidence, and those who lived [in faith] would live upon evidence."*
> (Qur'an, Al-Anfāl 8:42)

Thus, every reward and every punishment in the Hereafter is a **perfect reflection** of lived reality.

4. The Spiritual Effects of Knowing Life Is a Test

The one who grasps this truth lives differently:

- He walks with awareness, seeing every moment as a trial of integrity.
- He meets hardship with patience, and blessing with humility.
- He measures success not by wealth or status, but by sincerity and obedience.
- He avoids distraction and prepares for the meeting with God.

But the one who forgets this lives aimlessly, blinds himself to truth, and wastes life in a pursuit of shadows.

Recognizing life as a test **reshapes every thought, interaction, and priority**.

Conclusion

Life is not a random event—it is an **exam written by divine wisdom**.

- We advance in it through remembrance and righteous action,
- Or we regress through heedlessness and disobedience.

Everything we see, experience, and desire is part of this test—
part of the great examination sheet that will be opened on the Day of Judgment.

"[He] who created death and life to test you—which of you is best in deed."
   (Qur'an, Al-Mulk 67:2)

So live with intention.

   Act with clarity.

   And walk your days with the awareness that every choice brings you closer—

   either to eternal joy, or to eternal regret.

Racing Toward Good Deeds and Fulfilling Servitude

Introduction

In Islam, life is not defined by minimal religious duty,
   but by the **active pursuit of excellence in faith and action**.
   Human existence is elevated through **earnest striving**—a continuous
effort to embody servitude to God not only in obligation,
   but in intention, conduct, and initiative.

   "So race to [all that is] good."
      (Qur'an, Al-Baqarah 2:148)

   *"And the servants of the Most Merciful are those who walk upon the
   earth humbly..."*
      (Qur'an, Al-Furqān 25:63)

1. The Meaning of Competing in Goodness

To **strive in righteousness** (*istibāq al-khayrāt*) means:

- Hastening to acts of obedience before opportunities vanish.
- Engaging in noble competition—not for status, but for nearness to God.
- Initiating charity, justice, and reform without hesitation or delay.

In Islam, goodness is not to be awaited—it is to be pursued with the urgency of one running a race.

> *"It is they who hasten to good deeds, and they are foremost in them."*
> *(Qur'an, Al-Mu'minūn 23:61)*

2. Servitude in Action: How Striving Reflects 'Ubūdiyyah

Servitude (*'ubūdiyyah*) is not confined to ritual;
it is a **lifestyle of submission** in thought, will, and deed.
Racing toward good is the **living proof** of true servitude, for it reflects:

- Total **devotion**—placing God's pleasure above all.
- Eagerness to earn His love—through humility, generosity, and justice.
- Conscious use of time—recognizing that life is finite and purpose is eternal.

The sincere servant does not coast through life.
He walks with intention, competes with the heart, and rises with deeds—not slogans.

3. The Fields of Virtuous Competition

The race toward divine pleasure spans all areas of life:

- **Worship** – prayer, fasting, remembrance, and supplication.
- **Character** – truthfulness, patience, compassion, and trustworthiness.
- **Knowledge** – seeking, teaching, and applying what benefits the soul and others.
- **Social impact** – enjoining good, standing against injustice, serving the community.

Any action sincerely done for God becomes part of the race toward Him.

4. The Rewards of Striving in Goodness

To hasten toward good is to live with meaning—and to leave behind a legacy that pleases God and uplifts others.

Such a person:

- Lives by divine standards, not fleeting cultural trends.
- Finds blessings in both inner peace and outer consequence.
- Earns honor in this world and high station in the next.
- Becomes a **pillar in the construction of a righteous society**.

But whoever delays, hesitates, or clings to comfort—
squanders the rare and irreplaceable gift of time.

Conclusion

To race toward good is to live as one who truly understands life's purpose.
    It is the active fulfillment of servitude, the daily path of elevation, and the surest way to attain nearness to God.

"Indeed, those who hasten to good deeds—they are the ones brought near."

(Qur'an, Al-Wāqiʿah 56:10)

Whoever hastens to good **lives with clarity,**
   acts with conviction,
   and **prepares for eternity**—
not with passivity, but with a heart that runs toward its Lord.

IV

Death, the Grave, and the Barzakh — The Unseen Journey

Death, in the Islamic worldview, is not the end but a profound transition into the unseen—a passage that marks the beginning of a new phase in the human journey. It leads to the grave, the first station of the Hereafter, where the soul encounters questioning and experiences the initial unveiling of truth. Beyond the grave lies the Barzakh, a unique realm between two lives, serving as a preparatory stage that reflects a person's deeds and awaits the final resurrection. This unseen journey deepens our awareness of mortality, accountability, and the continuity of the soul beyond worldly life.

The Soul's Journey Beyond This World

Introduction

When the human being completes his journey through this world—from birth to the final breath—

a moment inevitably arrives: **a moment of transition**, unlike anything that has come before.

In the Islamic worldview, **death is not the end of existence**,

but the beginning of a new, unseen phase in the human journey.

It is the gateway to a realm beyond perception,

unfolding through the stages of the **Barzakh**, the **Resurrection**, and ultimately, **the eternal destiny**.

> *"Every soul shall taste death."*
> *(Qur'an, Āl ʿImrān 3:185)*

In this section of our journey, we will explore:

- The **reality of death** — its essence, wisdom, and inevitability.
- The **experience of the grave** — the first station of the afterlife, and the scene of questioning, comfort, or punishment.
- The **stage of the Barzakh** — the intermediate realm between this world and the Hereafter, filled with awareness and anticipation.

1. Death — The Inevitable Passage

Death is the first crossing from the **visible world to the unseen realm**.
It is not the annihilation of the soul,
but a **separation** of body and spirit—
a transition into the next stage of divine accounting.
It is the **first reality** of the afterlife, and the beginning of a phase in which the soul becomes fully aware of what lies ahead.

2. The Grave — The First Station of the Afterlife

The grave is not merely a burial site.
It is the first environment of recompense.

- For the righteous, it becomes a **garden from the gardens of Paradise**.
- For the rebellious, it becomes a **pit from the pits of Hellfire**.

The soul is returned to the body in a **barzakhī (interworldly) manner**,
and the questioning begins:
"Who is your Lord? What is your religion? Who is your Prophet?"
This is not symbolic—it is a **true experience** for the soul, whose state reflects the life it lived.

3. The Barzakh — Life Between This World and the Hereafter

From the grave, the soul enters the next stretch of its journey: **the Barzakh**.

This is the intermediate world stretching from death until the Day of Resurrection.

In the Barzakh:

- The soul remains **aware, conscious, and responsive**.
- It **tastes bliss or punishment**, based on its earthly deeds.
- It awaits resurrection with **longing or dread**, depending on what lies ahead.

"The Fire, they are exposed to it morning and evening, and on the Day the Hour is established: 'Admit the people of Pharaoh into the severest punishment.'"
  (Qur'an, Ghāfir 40:46)

The Barzakh is not idle—it is a phase of **anticipation, consequence, and continued awareness**.

4. The Spiritual Significance of This Phase

Together, **death, the grave, and the Barzakh** form a decisive triad—
  a period in which a person's eternal direction becomes known,
  even before the final reckoning.

- Those who lived with sincerity and repentance will find comfort, light, and divine nearness.
- Those who lived with heedlessness or defiance will taste separation, fear, and pre-judgment torment.

This phase is a **mirror of one's worldly life**, stripped of pretense and illusion.

A Call to Deep Reflection

Pause. Reflect.

Your book of deeds is still being written—but one day, the pen will stop.

Your limbs still act—but one day, they will rest in silence.

And beyond that moment begins a phase **longer, deeper, and more consequential** than everything that came before.

What lies ahead is not myth—it is reality.

It is waiting. And it is near.

So let us prepare—consciously and earnestly—for this immense transition.

Let us understand what awaits the soul in the unseen realm that stretches between **this fleeting world** and **the eternal one**.

Death — The Passage into the Unseen

Introduction

Death is the inescapable cosmic truth—the doorway every soul must cross.

It is the first gateway between the visible, worldly life and the unseen, eternal realm.

It makes no distinction between rich and poor, strong and weak, young and old.

Death marks the end of human agency and the beginning of divine reckoning.

It is the moment when the journey through the **abode of action** concludes, and the journey through the **abode of recompense** begins.

> *"Every soul shall taste death."*
> *(Qur'an, Āl 'Imrān 3:185)*

In the Islamic worldview, death is not a tragic conclusion,

but the **beginning of the next stage** in the human being's grand journey toward eternity.

119

1. The Nature of Death

Death is:

- The departure of the soul from the body,
- The loss of capacity to interact with the seen world (ʿālam al-shahādah),
- The entry into a new, unseen phase of existence.

It is not the end of life, but the **transition of the soul** to another realm: the realm of the **Barzakh**, where the soul awaits the final resurrection.

> *"Then indeed, after that you will surely die. Then indeed, you will be resurrected on the Day of Resurrection."*
> *(Qur'an, Al-Mu'minūn 23:15–16)*

2. The Inevitability of Death

Death is universal, unescapable, and precisely appointed.

- No soul, no matter its strength or knowledge, is exempt.
- It comes at its decreed time—neither delayed nor brought forward.
- Only God knows when it will arrive.

> *"Wherever you may be, death will overtake you—even if you are within towers of lofty construction."*
> *(Qur'an, An-Nisāʾ 4:78)*

This certainty is not meant to induce despair, but to awaken responsibility and humility in the human heart.

3. The Wisdom Behind Death

If death is certain, it is also purposeful.

- It strips the illusion of permanence from this world.
- It preserves divine justice—ensuring that eternal reward or punishment is reserved for the Hereafter.
- It closes the door to action and opens the door to **unveiled truth**.

Death is thus part of a **comprehensive divine order**,
  one that upholds justice, reveals truth, and inspires moral urgency.

4. The Moment of Death — A Decisive Encounter

When death arrives:

- The veil is lifted, and the unseen becomes visible.
- The soul sees the angels—either of mercy or punishment.
- The soul begins to experience the **initial phase of its destiny**: comfort or torment, serenity or dread.

> "Then, if he is of those brought near [to Allah], there is rest and bounty and a garden of delight."
>   (Qur'an, Al-Wāqi'ah 56:88–89)

And elsewhere:

> "Indeed, those who have said, 'Our Lord is Allah' and then remained steadfast—the angels descend upon them, [saying], 'Do not fear and do not grieve, but receive good tidings of Paradise which you were promised.'"

(Qur'an, Fuṣṣilat 41:30)

For this reason, the righteous across generations lived with a **constant awareness of death,**

preparing through sincere repentance, remembrance, and righteous deeds.

5. The Proper Attitude Toward Death

Islam does not call for fear-driven pessimism about death.

Rather, it commands **mindful preparation** and spiritual clarity.

- Live with intention, seeking to please God.
- Remember the fleeting nature of life.
- Maintain hope in God's mercy, while fearing a heedless end.

The Prophet ﷺ said:

> "Increase your remembrance of the destroyer of pleasures [i.e., death]."
> (Narrated by al-Tirmidhī)

To remember death is to **liberate the soul—**

from illusion, from arrogance, and from spiritual laziness.

It revives sincerity and renews purpose.

Conclusion

Death is the inevitable passage into the realm of ultimate reality.

It is the **turning point** that separates a life of trial from a life of judgment.

- Whoever prepares for it with faith and good deeds will find divine mercy in that moment.

• Whoever lives in distraction will be overtaken by death unaware—and will face regret too late to amend.

So let the believer welcome death not as a tragic end,
   but as the moment of meeting God,
   and the **beginning of eternal life**—the life for which we were always destined.

The Reality of Death in the Islamic Worldview

Introduction

In the Islamic worldview, death is not the absolute end that materialist thought suggests,

nor the vague and unknowable enigma posited by secular philosophies.

Rather, it is a **necessary existential reality**—

deeply woven into the divine design of life,

full of wisdom, and inseparably linked to the human being's purpose and destiny.

> *"Every soul shall taste death."*
> *(Qur'an, Āl 'Imrān 3:185)*

1. Death Is a Transition, Not Annihilation

According to Islamic teaching:

- Death is not the annihilation of the human being.
- It is a **transition** from one mode of existence to another.

At the moment of death:

- The soul departs from the body.
- The human being's engagement with the physical world ends.
- The soul enters the **Barzakh**—a realm of continued awareness, awaiting resurrection.

> *"And behind them is a barrier (Barzakh) until the Day they are resurrected."*
> *(Qur'an, Al-Mu'minūn 23:100)*

Thus, death is a **transformation**, not a cessation. It is not the end of the soul's story—only the end of its earthly chapter.

2. Death as Part of the Cycle of Creation

Death is not accidental or chaotic.

It is a **divinely created phase**—an integral part of the grand design of existence:

- God created both life and death as instruments of testing and refinement.
- Through them, the soul journeys from creation to resurrection, from trial to recompense.

> *"[He] who created death and life to test you [as to] which of you is best in deed."*
> *(Qur'an, Al-Mulk 67:2)*

Death is therefore not a breakdown of the divine plan,
but a **necessary station** in a journey ordained by wisdom.

3. Death as a Manifestation of God's Mercy and Justice

- Death is **mercy**, because it ends the human being's exposure to worldly suffering and trial.
- Death is **justice**, because it leads to a realm where **every soul receives its due**.

Without death, there would be no Day of Judgment,
   and oppression would remain unpunished, while virtue might go unrewarded.
   Thus, death opens the gate to ultimate fairness—
   a **hidden blessing** within the structure of divine mercy and accountability.

4. Death as the Unveiling of the Soul's Reality

At the moment of death, the veil is lifted.

- The soul sees the reality it once believed in or denied.
- The truth of one's faith, sincerity, and inner state is made plain.
- There is no longer illusion, pretense, or denial—only clarity.

> *"So We have removed from you your covering, and your sight this Day is sharp."*
>   *(Qur'an, Qāf 50:22)*

In this moment, the human being is sorted—between those whose hearts were upright and those who lived in heedlessness.
   Death reveals what life often conceals.

5. The Required Attitude Toward Death

Islamic guidance calls for a balanced stance:

- **Conscious fear** that awakens repentance and vigilance.
- **Hope in God's mercy**, knowing that He forgives the sincere.
- **Seriousness in life**, rooted in the awareness of its brief and sacred nature.

The Prophet ﷺ said:

> "Increase your remembrance of the destroyer of pleasures [i.e., death]."
>
> (Narrated by al-Tirmidhī)

This remembrance is not meant to induce despair—
but to **free the soul from illusion** and anchor it in purpose.

Conclusion

In the Islamic perspective, death is not a meaningless end.

- It is **not annihilation**, but continuation in a new, conscious form.
- It is **not injustice**, but part of a greater system of mercy and justice.
- It is **not an enigma**, but a revealed reality illuminated by divine scripture.

Whoever prepares for death walks toward eternity with **light and certainty**.
But whoever ignores it will awaken in regret,
having lost both this world and the next.
Let death be to the believer not a shadow of fear—
but a doorway to meeting the One who created him in truth.

Death as a New Beginning

Introduction

In the Islamic worldview, death is not the end of the human story,
  nor does it annihilate the soul or cast it into oblivion.
  Rather, it is the **beginning of a new stage of existence—**
  one that is greater, more expansive, and infinitely more enduring than
life in this world.

> *"Indeed, the Hereafter—that is the [true] life, if only they knew."*
>   *(Qur'an, Al-'Ankabūt 29:64)*

This world is temporary and incomplete. The life beyond it is the complete
and lasting reality.

1. Death: The Gateway to Barzakh

At the moment of death:

- The soul departs the body and enters the realm of the **Barzakh,**
- It begins a new phase of perception and spiritual awareness,
- It experiences the **initial consequences** of its deeds—either comfort
  or torment.

The Prophet ﷺ said:

> "The grave is either a garden from the gardens of Paradise or a pit from the pits of Hell."
> (Narrated by al-Tirmidhī)

Thus, death is not a fall into silence or nonexistence—
   it is the opening of a door into **a different mode of life**: unseen, yet more real.

2. Death: The Unveiling of Hidden Truths

At the threshold of death, the veils are lifted.

- One sees the angels—welcoming or dreading.
- One witnesses the reality of divine recompense.
- One becomes certain of what was once believed or doubted.

> *"So We have removed your covering, and your sight today is sharp."*
> *(Qur'an, Qāf 50:22)*

Death marks the **transition from the world of belief to the world of certainty**.
   It is no longer a matter of faith—it becomes vision.

3. Death: The Start of Rise or Fall

Death is not a neutral event. It is the moment of spiritual divergence:

- The believer begins his **ascent**—into mercy, light, and peace.
- The denier or wrongdoer begins a **descent**—into regret, darkness, and isolation.

> *"Indeed, those who have said, 'Our Lord is Allah' and then remained steadfast—the angels descend upon them [saying], 'Do not fear and do not grieve, but receive glad tidings of Paradise which you were promised.'"*
>
> *(Qur'an, Fuṣṣilat 41:30)*

Thus, death is the **moment of divine sorting**,
   where destinies begin to unfold in accordance with one's earthly life.

4. Death: The Passage to Eternal Life

For the believer, death is not a defeat—it is liberation.

- A release from the limitations and trials of the body.
- An entry into the **realm of divine nearness and tranquility**.
- The beginning of a life with no pain, no loss, and no end.

The one who lived only for this world will see death as a tragedy.
   But the one who lived for God will see it as the **start of their return to Him**.

> *"But you prefer the worldly life, while the Hereafter is better and more enduring."*
>
> *(Qur'an, Al-Aʿlā 87:16–17)*

Conclusion

In the Islamic understanding, death is not a tragic ending.
   It is a **new beginning**—the start of the soul's most meaningful journey.

- It is the entrance to the **abode of truth**.

- It is the unveiling of the realities we held by faith.
- It is the beginning of **eternity**—in bliss or in sorrow.

So let the wise prepare for their greater birth:
the birth into the eternal life that begins when the soul departs this world.

The Grave — The First Abode of the Hereafter

Introduction

With death, a person closes the chapter of worldly life and enters the first stage of their unseen existence: **the grave**.

In the Islamic worldview, the grave is not merely a resting place for the body;

it is the **first station of the Hereafter,**

where the soul begins to experience the consequences of its deeds under the justice of God,

preparing for what lies beyond—**eternal life**.

The Prophet Muhammad ﷺ said:

> "The grave is the first station of the Hereafter. Whoever succeeds in it, what follows will be easier for him; and whoever fails in it, what follows will be more severe."
>
> (Narrated by al-Tirmidhī and Ibn Mājah)

1. The Grave: Entry into the Next Life

- The grave serves as a **gateway into Barzakh**, the intermediate realm between this world and the Resurrection.
- The soul reconnects with the body in a unique, interworldly manner—not as it did in worldly life, but in a state suited to the unseen.
- It is a place of **awareness, perception, and initial recompense**.

It is not a dormant void, but a conscious reality.

> *"So the evil consequences of what they earned struck them, and that which they used to ridicule encompassed them."*
> (Qur'an, Az-Zumar 39:48)

This verse signals the beginning of divine justice in the realm beyond sight.

2. The Trial and Questioning of the Grave

When the soul is laid to rest, its trial begins with three pivotal questions:

- Who is your Lord?
- What is your religion?
- Who is your Prophet?

The Prophet ﷺ said:

> "When a servant is placed in his grave, and his companions leave him—he even hears the sound of their footsteps—two angels come to him..."
> (Narrated by al-Bukhārī and Muslim)

- The believer, through faith and sincerity, answers clearly and is honored.

- The disbeliever or hypocrite stumbles, unable to respond—his failure marking the start of torment.

3. Bliss or Punishment in the Grave

The result of this interrogation determines the soul's condition until the Day of Judgment:

- For the believer: **a garden from the gardens of Paradise**—filled with peace, light, and good news.
- For the defiant: **a pit from the pits of Hell**—filled with darkness, pressure, and fear.

> *"The Fire—they are exposed to it morning and evening."*
> *(Qur'an, Ghāfir 40:46)*

This verse affirms that punishment (or reward) in the grave is real, experienced continuously until the Resurrection.

Each soul resides in a condition of the grave that **mirrors their life's choices**—awaiting the final judgment.

4. The Grave as Prelude to Resurrection

The grave is not the end of the journey. It is a **temporary, conscious station** where initial consequences begin.

What follows is resurrection, judgment, and the eternal destiny.

> *"From it We created you, and into it We shall return you, and from it We shall bring you forth once more."*
> *(Qur'an, Ṭāhā 20:55)*

The body returns to earth, but the soul waits—aware, alert, and already living the early signs of its ultimate fate.

5. Lessons from the Reality of the Grave

- The remembrance of the grave breaks pride and softens the heart.
- It motivates sincere action and detaches the soul from worldly illusions.

The Prophet ﷺ said:

> "I had previously forbidden you from visiting graves. Now visit
> them, for they remind you of the Hereafter."
> (Narrated by Muslim)

To visit the graves is to **remember your own destination**,
and to reflect upon what truly lasts beyond this world.

Conclusion

The grave is the first true test of the Hereafter.

- **For the one who prepared with faith and good deeds**, it will be
filled with light and serenity.
- **For the one who lived in heedlessness**, it will be dark, tight, and
terrifying.

Let the mindful and rational person prepare for this decisive station—
before the body returns to dust and the pen is lifted.
Let every day be a conscious step toward **a radiant grave**,
and a blessed eternity.

The Grave Questioning and the Encounter with the Unseen

Introduction

From the moment a person is laid in their grave,
  they transition from the world of the seen—which they once knew—
  to the unseen realm they either believed in or denied.
  Here begins the first decisive trial of the soul after death:
  the Grave Questioning (*fitnat al-qabr*).
  This moment marks the beginning of direct encounter with ultimate truths,
  a moment when belief is tested not by memory, but by the condition of the heart.
  It is the unveiling of what one lived for, and the affirmation of a soul's path before resurrection and final judgment.

1. The Nature of the Grave Questioning

According to rigorously authenticated Prophetic reports:

- Two angels—**Munkar and Nakīr**—are sent to the deceased.
- They seat the soul and ask **three fundamental questions**:

1. Who is your Lord?
2. What is your religion?
3. Who is your Prophet?

These questions are not surface-level examinations.

They expose the **core identity** of the soul: its allegiance, belief, and lived values.

2. The Nature of the Response

- The true believer answers with ease and confidence:

"My Lord is Allah."
 "My religion is Islam."
 "My prophet is Muhammad ﷺ."

> *"Allah keeps firm those who believe, with the firm word, in worldly life and in the Hereafter."*
>   *(Qur'an, Ibrāhīm 14:27)*

- The hypocrite or disbeliever responds with confusion and regret:

"Haah, haah... I don't know."
 Or they offer empty slogans devoid of spiritual substance.
 This moment does not reward memorized answers,
 but **reveals the authenticity** of one's faith and orientation in life.

3. The Purpose of the Grave Questioning

This trial is not a theological quiz; it is a soul's disclosure.

1. It exposes whether the person lived as a **servant of God** or a **slave to**

the self.

2. It confirms their coming state:

- The one who answers with conviction is **prepared for bliss**,
- The one who stumbles is **set up for punishment**.

It proves that faith is not theoretical knowledge,
    but a living reality rooted in **the heart, supported by deeds**, and manifest at the moment of truth.

4. Experiencing the Unseen: The Life of Barzakh

From the moment of questioning:

- The soul begins its **conscious experience of the unseen**.
- It perceives realities once hidden: angels, spirits, and signs of its eternal fate.
- It lives in a state of **awareness corresponding to its earthly deeds**—rewarded or punished until the Day of Resurrection.

As some scholars have said:
    "Whoever dies, their personal resurrection has begun."
    The grave is not unconsciousness; it is **Barzakh life**—infused with perception, presence, and consequence.

5. Living with Awareness of the Grave Questioning

Those who internalize the reality of this trial:

- Strengthen their **creed** and cultivate **sincere faith**,
- Strive for **purity of intention** and guard against hypocrisy,
- Treat every act of worship and every moral decision as a preparation for this moment.

They understand that **outward rituals are not enough**—what matters is the soul's alignment with God.

The righteous among the early generations would often pray:

"O Allah, make us firm at the time of death and in the grave."

Conclusion

The Grave Questioning is the soul's first unveiling—

its confrontation with the truths it once **professed**, **neglected**, or **rejected**.

- Allah strengthens those who believed and lived sincerely.
- The hypocrite is left to his confusion, exposed by a heart that lacked conviction.

Whoever prepares for this decisive moment

will be protected from its terror,

settled by divine peace,

and begin the journey to eternal bliss beneath the shade of God's mercy.

Barzakh — The Life Between Two Lives

Introduction

After passing through the stages of death and the grave,
the human being enters a hidden but real phase of existence: **Barzakh**.

In the Islamic worldview, Barzakh is neither annihilation nor unconscious void.

It is a distinct mode of life—**situated between the world of action and the world of final judgment**—
imbued with awareness, emotion, and early manifestations of divine recompense.

> *"And behind them is a barrier (Barzakh) until the Day they are resurrected."*
> *(Qur'an, Al-Mu'minūn 23:100)*

1. Definition of Barzakh

Linguistically, *Barzakh* means a barrier—something that separates two entities.

Theologically, it refers to:
The intermediate life that begins at death and continues until the Resurrection.

140

Barzakh is not part of the temporal world, nor is it the complete Hereafter. It is a **transitional realm**, governed by its own laws, designed to reveal a soul's standing with God.

2. Characteristics of Life in Barzakh

Life in Barzakh is marked by several defining features:

- **Continuity**: It endures until the Day of Resurrection.
- **Awareness**: The soul perceives, reacts, and experiences—either bliss or torment.
- **Preliminary Recompense**: The soul begins to taste its eternal fate based on past deeds.
- **Timelessness**: Time is experienced differently—centuries may feel like moments, or moments like an eternity.

Barzakh is real life—hidden, conscious, and morally consequential.

3. Barzakh as a Stage of Initial Recompense

In this phase:

- The **believer** is shown their place in Paradise and tastes its comfort.
- The **disbeliever** and the corrupt soul begin to suffer a foretaste of divine punishment.

The Prophet Muhammad ﷺ said:

> "When one of you dies, his place in Paradise or Hell is shown to him morning and evening…"
> (Agreed upon: al-Bukhārī and Muslim)

Barzakh is thus a **prelude to the Final Judgment**, offering a preview of

141

what is to come.

4. Conscious Experience Between Bliss and Torment

Barzakh is not static—it reflects the soul's deeds:

- **Righteous souls** may be comforted, rejoice in their reward, and even encounter other righteous souls.
- **Wicked souls** may be confined, punished, or grieved—cut off from light and ease.
- The souls of **martyrs**, for example, roam freely in Paradise.
- The souls of **wrongdoers** may be detained and chastised.

Barzakh is the stage where the **truth of a person's life begins to unfold** in experiential form.

5. Living in Awareness of Barzakh

Belief in Barzakh should shape earthly life. It:

- Instills a deep sense of **moral accountability**.
- Cures spiritual **heedlessness** that arises from the illusion that death ends our story.
- Encourages sincerity, humility, and action—knowing that the soul's journey continues immediately after death.

"Whoever dies, their personal resurrection has begun."
Every act today will echo in Barzakh—whether in comfort or regret.

6. Barzakh and the Greater Afterlife

Barzakh is not the final destination.

It is a **conscious waiting station**, where the soul undergoes early reward or punishment while awaiting:

- **Resurrection,**
- **Judgment,**
- And **entry into Paradise or Hell**.

Its conditions—though real—are temporary.

The full fate of every soul will be made manifest only on the Day of Standing.

Conclusion

Barzakh is the second great phase of human life,
and the **first step into conscious eternity**.

- It distinguishes souls by their creed and conduct.
- It begins the harvest of one's worldly journey.
- It sets the tone for the soul's final fate.

Whoever prepared for this realm through faith, sincerity, and righteous action
will find comfort, peace, and the early light of Paradise.
But whoever lived in heedlessness
will encounter torment and loneliness—
even before the greater judgment has begun.
Let us live today with eyes turned toward what lies between the grave and eternity.

Barzakh as a Preparatory Stage

Introduction

In the Islamic worldview, **Barzakh is neither a final phase nor a place of eternal settlement**.

Rather, it is a preparatory station—**bridging the fleeting life of this world and the everlasting life of the Hereafter**.

It is a realm of transition and unveiling, where the soul begins to perceive the consequences of its earthly journey and is readied for the ultimate scene of judgment.

> *"And behind them is a barrier (Barzakh) until the Day they are resurrected."*
> *(Qur'an, Al-Mu'minūn 23:100)*

1. The Nature of Barzakh as an Intermediate Realm

Barzakh is distinct from both worldly life and the afterlife. It is a real domain with its own laws and spiritual topography:

- **Perception and Awareness**: The soul is aware, though not in the sensory-bound way of this world.
- **Partial Recompense**: It includes reward and punishment, though not

the full bliss of Paradise or the total agony of Hell.
- **Altered Time**: Time flows differently—compressed, expanded, or suspended relative to earthly measures.

Though it lies between two realms, Barzakh is not a symbolic abstraction; it is a **serious, conscious phase** of the human journey.

2. The Preparatory Functions of Barzakh

Barzakh serves critical existential purposes that begin shaping the soul's eternal outcome:

Initial Recompense:

- The believer experiences glimpses of divine comfort.
- The disbeliever and sinner begin to feel the weight of punishment.

Spiritual Exposure:

- The faithful are made firm, receiving glad tidings and peace.
- The heedless encounter humiliation, regret, and unrest.

Foreshadowing Destiny:

- What unfolds in Barzakh previews the final outcome on the Day of Resurrection.

Barzakh is not final judgment, but it gives the soul its first real taste of where it is headed.

3. Barzakh as Psychological and Spiritual Preparation

During Barzakh, the inner states of the soul intensify:

- The **believer's** serenity deepens as they anticipate the meeting with their Lord.
- The **disbeliever's** pain is compounded by clarity, regret, and helplessness.

The soul is thus prepared—emotionally, spiritually, and morally—for the unveiling of divine justice on the Day of Resurrection.

4. Barzakh as a Barrier Between Two Realms

Barzakh functions as a veil—separating the living from the dead, and the world of action from the world of recompense.

> *"Until, when death comes to one of them, he says, 'My Lord, return me so I may do good in what I left behind.' Never! It is only a word he is saying. And behind them is a barrier until the Day they are resurrected."*
> *(Qur'an, Al-Mu'minūn 23:99–100)*

- There is no return to this world once Barzakh begins.
- There is no crossing into the Hereafter until the Final Resurrection.

Barzakh locks the door of action and opens the gate of consequences.

5. Barzakh and the Continuing Impact of Earthly Deeds

Though personal deeds end at death, their effects may continue:

- **Ongoing charity (ṣadaqah jāriyah),**
- **Beneficial knowledge left behind,**
- **Righteous children who pray for the deceased.**

Barzakh becomes a field where the fruits of past efforts **continue to ripen**—either sweet or bitter—until the Day of Judgment.

Conclusion

Barzakh is not an interruption in the soul's journey—**it is its unveiling**.

- It marks the soul's first encounter with the unseen.
- It previews reward or punishment with unmistakable clarity.
- It prepares the soul for the final reckoning by drawing back the veil between belief and reality.

Whoever enters Barzakh with light, faith, and good deeds will find reassurance and divine mercy.

But whoever enters it heedless, hollow, or rebellious will face darkness, isolation, and bitter regret.

Let every moment of this life be preparation—

not only for death,

but for the **life between two lives**.

V

Resurrection and Judgment — The Unveiling of Truth

Resurrection and Judgment mark the ultimate unveiling of truth, when all of creation is brought forth on the Day of Resurrection—a day of cosmic upheaval, awe-inspiring scenes, and absolute justice. It is the moment when every soul stands before God, witnessing the full presentation of their deeds, with nothing hidden or forgotten. This is the Day of Reckoning, where divine justice is perfectly administered, and each person is judged by clear standards of faith, sincerity, and righteous action—leading either to eternal reward or rightful consequence.

When All Truths Are Revealed

Introduction

After the silence of Barzakh has passed,
   and souls reach the end of their waiting,
   a cosmic trumpet will sound—
   and the entire universe will move toward a moment of unmatched awe
and finality:

The Day of Resurrection.

It is a day of upheaval and transformation:
   The earth is reshaped, the heavens split open, graves burst forth,
   and every soul stands before its Creator for the **Great Reckoning**.

> *"On the Day when the earth will be changed to another earth, and
> the heavens [as well], and they will appear before Allah, the One, the
> Irresistible."*
> *(Qur'an, Ibrāhīm 14:48)*

151

1. Resurrection — A Cosmic Overturning and Revelation of Truth

Resurrection is not merely the return of bodies from the dust—
it is a complete unraveling of the physical order as we know it.
It is the day when **the unseen becomes seen**,
when the truths once held in faith or dismissed in arrogance
are displayed with unmistakable clarity.
All veils fall.
All illusions end.
It is the Day when every soul faces reality without filter or escape.

2. Judgment — The Moment of Revealing Deeds and Intentions

On this Day, the justice of God is fully unveiled:

- Every deed—major or minor—is presented with precision.
- The earth speaks. The limbs testify. Nothing is hidden.

> *"On that Day, it will report its news — because your Lord will have inspired it."*
> *(Qur'an, Az-Zalzalah 99:4–5)*

Each person will receive their record:

- **In the right hand**, for those destined to succeed.
- **In the left**, for those doomed by their choices.

Even unspoken intentions, hidden motives, and silent thoughts are made visible.

3. Resurrection and Judgment as the Fulfillment of Divine Justice

But Judgment is not merely about exposure—
it is the fulfillment of divine justice in its most complete form.

- No oppressor escapes.
- No victim is forgotten.
- No soul is wronged by even an atom's weight.

> *"We shall set up the scales of justice for the Day of Resurrection, so that no soul will be wronged in the least."*
> *(Qur'an, Al-Anbiyā' 21:47)*

This is the moment where **absolute justice** is done—
a justice no court on earth could ever replicate,
a justice only the All-Knowing, All-Wise Judge can render.

The Centrality of This Section

Resurrection and Judgment are the **pinnacle of the human journey**.

- Here, every act finds its full meaning.
- Here, destinies are sealed—Paradise or Hell, joy or regret.
- Here, faith is no longer a claim, but a verdict.

What began as a test ends as a reckoning.

A Call for Reflection and Readiness

This chapter is not merely for reflection—
it is a call to awakening:

- To prepare for the day when inner secrets will be made public.
- To treat every moment as a step toward meeting the One who knows us best.

Let us prepare for the Day

> *"when neither wealth nor children will benefit,*
> *except for one who comes to Allah with a sound heart."*
> *(Qur'an, Ash-Shu'arā' 26:88–89)*

Let us live now with the truth in view—
so that when the veils fall,
we are not among those who meet that Day with regret,
but among those who meet it with light, peace, and God's eternal pleasure.

The Day of Resurrection — The Day of Cosmic Overturning

Introduction

The **Day of Resurrection** is the most decisive moment in the history of creation—
   when time collapses, veils fall, and all truth is laid bare.
   It is the day that marks the end of the material world and the beginning of the eternal realm,
   when the cosmic order is shattered to make way for the final unveiling:
   Resurrection, Judgment, and Recompense.

> *"When the earth is shaken with its [final] earthquake, and the earth discharges its burdens..."*
> *(Qur'an, Az-Zalzalah 99:1–2)*

1. Cosmic Upheaval — The Collapse of Creation

The moment the Hour is established is marked by unimaginable cataclysm:

- The earth quakes with a violent trembling.
- Mountains crumble and scatter like wool.

- The stars are extinguished. The sky is torn. Oceans boil and spill forth.
- All structures of earthly life dissolve.

> "On the Day the quaking blast will convulse [everything], followed by the subsequent blast."
> (Qur'an, An-Nāziʿāt 79:6– 7)

The universe, once governed by stability, now collapses in submission to divine command—

making way for a **new order of existence**.

2. The Trumpet — Death and Resurrection in Two Blows

The Resurrection begins with the **blowing of the Trumpet**—a sound that will echo across all realms of creation.

The first blow:

- All living beings fall into unconsciousness.
- Life ceases across the heavens and the earth, save for whom Allah wills.

The second blow:

- Humanity is resurrected.
- Souls are reunited with their bodies.
- All are raised to stand for judgment.

"And the trumpet will be blown, and all who are in the heavens and the earth will fall unconscious, except whom Allah wills. Then it will be blown again, and at once they will be standing, looking on."
(Qur'an, Az-Zumar 39:68)

This is the moment where silence ends, and reckoning begins.

3. The Gathering — Where All Stand as Equals

- From every grave, the dead emerge—barefoot, naked, and uncircumcised.
- The sun descends close. The intensity of the moment causes sweat to rise in proportion to one's deeds.
- Fear silences every tongue. No privilege remains.

The Prophet ﷺ said:

> "You will be gathered barefoot, naked, and uncircumcised."
> (Agreed upon)

On that Plain of Gathering, **kings and beggars**, **scholars and tyrants**, **the mighty and the meek—**
all stand on equal ground, awaiting their eternal verdict.

4. Divine Truth Over Worldly Illusion

In the worldly life, false standards prevailed:

- Power often triumphed over justice.
- Wealth overshadowed principle.
- Desire disguised itself as truth.

But on this Day, all illusions collapse:

157

> *"Then when the trumpet is blown, no relationships will remain between them that Day, nor will they ask about one another."*
> *(Qur'an, Al-Mu'minūn 23:101)*

- Lineage will not save.
- Prestige will not speak.
- Wealth will be weightless.

Only faith, sincerity, and righteous action will hold value.

5. The Terror of the Moment and the Solitary Soul

The terror of that Day will overwhelm every soul.

- Parents will flee from their children.
- Friends will abandon each other.
- Each person will be consumed by their own fate.

> *"On the Day a man will flee from his brother, and his mother and his father, and his wife and his children."*
> *(Qur'an, 'Abasa 80:34–36)*

The only ones who remain composed are those whom Allah shields with His mercy—
those who prepared for this meeting in the short days of the worldly life.

Conclusion

The Day of Resurrection is not merely the end of life as we know it—
it is the grand unveiling of the truth of existence.

- It is the day where secrets are revealed and justice is absolute.
- It is the day where falsehood vanishes, and every soul is shown what it truly earned.

"So let every soul look to what it has sent ahead for tomorrow."
(Qur'an, Al-Hashr 59:18)

Let each heartbeat be a reminder of that coming Day.
Let each deed reflect the weight of that eternal moment.
Whoever lives with it in mind walks toward divine mercy.
Whoever ignores it walks blind into their fate.

The Great Scenes of the Day of Resurrection

Introduction

The **Day of Resurrection** is not a single instant, nor a fleeting moment of reckoning.

It is a vast, awe-inspiring unfolding of events—one scene after another—each carrying its own weight, fear, and majesty.

It is the day when the cosmos collapses and is reformed,

when illusions are stripped away and only truth remains.

It is the day when divine justice is revealed in full.

> *"Then how will you fear, if you persist in disbelief, a Day that will make the hair of children white?"*
> (Qur'an, Al-Muzzammil 73:17)

Every scene on that Day reveals what was once hidden—until nothing is left but pure, divine reality.

1. The Collapse of Creation — The First Trumpet Blast

The first trumpet announces the end of the created world:

- All living beings fall unconscious.
- The heavens and the earth are shattered.
- Stars vanish, oceans boil, mountains crumble like wool.

"And the trumpet will be blown, and whoever is in the heavens and whoever is on the earth will fall dead..."
(Qur'an, Az-Zumar 39:68)

This is no metaphor—it is the total dissolution of the known universe.

2. The Awakening — The Second Trumpet and Resurrection

After a period known only to God, the trumpet is blown again.

- Graves break open.
- Souls are reunited with their bodies.
- People rise barefoot, naked, and uncircumcised, stunned by the immensity of what lies ahead.

"Then it will be blown again, and behold—they will be standing, looking on."
(Qur'an, Az-Zumar 39:68)

The dead are no longer dead. Every soul is brought back to life—to witness and be witnessed.

3. The Gathering — On the Plain of Assembly

All of creation is driven to a new land: flat, featureless, and vast.

There are no mountains, no shade—just the blazing sun drawn close overhead.

- People sweat in proportion to their sins.
- Some are drowning, others shaded by their deeds.

The Prophet ﷺ said:

> "Seven will be shaded by Allah in His shade on a day when there
> is no shade but His…"
>   (*Agreed upon*)

Each soul stands isolated—waiting for judgment, stripped of title, status, and worldly protection.

4. The Exposure — Standing Before God and the Records Unveiled

The reckoning begins.

- Deeds are presented in totality—nothing is omitted or forgotten.
- Limbs speak. Tongues bear witness.
- The earth itself testifies.

> *"That Day it will report its news."*
>   (Qur'an, Az-Zalzalah 99:4)

The faithful receive their records in their right hands.

The deniers receive theirs in their left—or from behind.

It is the moment where every secret becomes public.

5. The Scales of Justice — Weighing the Deeds

The divine scales are established with perfect precision.

> *"And We will set up the scales of justice for the Day of Resurrection, so no soul will be wronged in the least."*
> (Qur'an, Al-Anbiya 21:47)

- Good deeds are weighed against evil.
- Even the smallest act—an atom's weight—is not overlooked.
- The outcome is just. There is no appeal.

This is not a trial—it is the final audit of the soul.

6. The Grand Intercession — The Compassion of the Chosen Ones

In the midst of dread and waiting, the Prophet Muhammad ﷺ will be granted the **Great Intercession**.

- He will plead for the judgment to begin.
- Other prophets, martyrs, and righteous people will intercede—with Allah's permission only.

> *"Who is it that can intercede with Him except by His permission?"*
> (Qur'an, Al-Baqarah 2:255)

This intercession is not a bypass of justice, but a manifestation of divine mercy.

7. The Sirat — The Final Bridge

A bridge is stretched across the Hellfire. It is thinner than a hair and sharper than a sword.

Every soul must cross:

- The righteous pass like lightning.
- The cautious walk step by step.
- The unrepentant stumble and fall.

This is the final trial. After the Sirat, only eternal reward or eternal loss remains.

Conclusion: The Day of Truth, the Day of Sorting

The Day of Resurrection is not a myth. It is the day **of unveiling, of divine justice, of irrevocable truth**.

- On that Day, **no soul will be wronged.**
- **No injustice will be left unaddressed.**
- **No refuge will exist except in God's mercy.**

> *"That Day, wealth and children will not benefit—except one who comes to Allah with a sound heart."*
> (Qur'an, Ash-Shu'arā 26:88–89)

Let each day in this world be preparation for that eternal day.
Let each deed be weighed now—before it is weighed then.

The Day of Perfect Balance: Divine Justice in the Hereafter

Introduction

Among the most awe-inspiring truths of the Day of Judgment in the Islamic worldview is the full unveiling of divine justice—a justice untouched by flaw, bias, or error. On that Day, God's knowledge, fairness, and power manifest in their most complete form, revealing the final outcome of every soul's choices.

> **"And your Lord is not ever unjust to the servants."**
> (Qur'an, Fussilat 41:46)

1. The Pillars of Divine Justice

Divine justice rests on three unshakable pillars, each revealing how no deed is overlooked, and no soul wronged:

1.1. Perfect Knowledge

Nothing escapes God's awareness. Every thought, whisper, and action—public or private—is known to Him.

> **"Indeed, Allah is Witness over all things."** (Qur'an, An-Nisa 4:33)

1.2. Precise Documentation

Each human being is accompanied by angels who record every deed with flawless accuracy.

> **"We bring forth for him on the Day of Resurrection a book spread open."** (Qur'an, Al-Isra 17:13)

1.3. Testimony Beyond Denial

On that Day, not even the body will protect its owner. Hands, feet, and tongue testify; even the earth recounts its history.

> **"On the Day when their tongues, hands, and feet will bear witness against them."** (Qur'an, An-Nur 24:24)

2. Justice Made Manifest: Principles in Action

This isn't theoretical justice—it is justice revealed through real consequences:

- **No punishment without prior warning:** Every nation received messengers. No soul is judged without having been shown the way.

"We never punish until We have sent a messenger." (Qur'an, Al-Isra 17:15)

- **Each soul judged by its capacity:** None is burdened beyond what they can bear.
- **Individual accountability:** No one carries another's sin. Each is held for their own record.

"No bearer of burdens shall bear the burden of another." (Qur'an, Al-An'am 6:164)

3. The Outcomes: Justice and Mercy Intertwined

- **Good is multiplied:** Even a small deed, done with sincerity, is met with abundance.
- **Evil is not exaggerated:** A sin is answered only with its due—never more.
- **God's mercy remains supreme:** He forgives whom He wills, accepts repentance, and overlooks much out of compassion.

"Indeed, your Lord is vast in forgiveness." (Qur'an, An-Najm 53:32)

This is not only justice—it is divine generosity within justice.

4. The Transformative Power of Belief in Divine Justice

To believe in divine justice is to reshape one's entire life:

- It instills peace, knowing that no right will be lost.
- It inspires accountability, as every action carries weight.
- It dissolves despair over worldly injustice, for the final word belongs to God alone.

Conclusion: A Day Without Injustice

The Day of Judgment is the day of perfect balance:

- No soul is overlooked.
- No injustice is done.
- No effort is lost.

> **"We will set up the scales of justice for the Day of Resurrection..."**
> (Qur'an, Al-Anbiya 21:47)

When all secrets are laid bare and every soul sees the truth of what it sent ahead, only those who lived with sincerity and foresight will rejoice.

So live with the certainty that justice awaits—perfect, unshakable, and near.

The Reckoning — The Moment of Truth

Introduction

After the awe-inspiring events of resurrection and gathering, the human being arrives at the most critical moment in their existence:

The Reckoning.

This is the moment when every veil is lifted, and the absolute truth is revealed:

- The truth of one's actions, both public and hidden.
- The sincerity or hypocrisy that marked one's intentions.
- The full weight of obedience or disobedience to God's commands.

"So whoever does an atom's weight of good will see it,
  And whoever does an atom's weight of evil will see it."
  (Qur'an, Az-Zalzalah 99:7–8)

1. The Meaning of Reckoning in the Islamic Worldview

The Reckoning (*ḥisāb*) refers to God's evaluation of each individual based on their beliefs, words, actions, and innermost intentions. It is:

- Comprehensive and exact—nothing, no matter how small, escapes it.
- A moment of ultimate clarity, where one's Book of Deeds is laid bare.
- A definitive turning point, when a person receives their record—
- In the right hand: a sign of divine pleasure and salvation.
- In the left hand: a sign of regret, disgrace, and ruin.

> *"Then as for he who is given his record in his right hand—*
> *He will be judged with an easy account."*
> (Qur'an, Al-Inshiqaq 84:7–8)

2. How the Reckoning Is Carried Out

a. Presentation of the Record

- Every deed is documented with divine precision.
- Witnesses are brought forth:
- A person's own limbs—hands, feet, eyes, and tongue.
- The angels who recorded each act.
- Even the earth testifies to what occurred upon it.

> *"On the Day when their tongues, their hands, and their feet will bear*
> *witness against them as to what they used to do."*
> (Qur'an, An-Nur 24:24)

b. Weighing on the Scales

- The *mīzān* (scales) are set, and each deed is weighed with perfect fairness.
- God's mercy may multiply a single good deed many times over.
- Sins are weighed, but never exaggerated.

c. Degrees of Reckoning

- Some believers are shown their sins, then pardoned—this is the *light reckoning*.
- Others face detailed questioning, a harrowing process that often leads to punishment.

The Prophet ﷺ said:

> "Whoever is held to account thoroughly will be punished."
> *(Agreed upon – Bukhari & Muslim)*

3. The Human Condition on the Day of Reckoning

a. The Upright Believer

- Secure in their faith.
- Judged with ease and entered into Paradise by God's mercy.

b. The Sinful Believer

- Brought to account for shortcomings.
- Outcome depends on repentance, forgiveness, and divine justice.

c. The Hypocrite and Disbeliever

- Their deception is exposed.
- Their deeds are nullified.
- Their fate is eternal loss.

> *"Here, read my record!"* (Al-Haqqah 69:19) — The joyful cry of the righteous.

> *"Oh, I wish I had not been given my record..."* (Al-Haqqah 69:25) — The lament of the condemned.

4. The Role of Belief in the Reckoning

Belief in the Reckoning is transformative:

- It instills reverence and accountability.
- It motivates moral integrity and humility.
- It encourages constant self-evaluation and repentance.
- It protects against arrogance and spiritual complacency.

The one who remembers the Reckoning lives deliberately—with every word and choice shaped by the awareness of standing before God.

5. Perfect Divine Justice

God's justice on the Day of Reckoning is flawless:

- No one is wronged.

- Every person is judged individually—no soul bears the burden of another.
- Even the smallest good or evil is acknowledged.

> *"Indeed, Allah does not wrong [even] as much as an atom's weight."*
> (Qur'an, An-Nisa 4:40)

Yet His justice is accompanied by mercy:

- Forgiveness is granted to those who repent.
- Good deeds are multiplied.
- Intercession is allowed for those whom God permits.

Conclusion:

The Reckoning is the final unveiling—where hearts are exposed and destinies sealed.

- The one who lived with sincerity, faith, and humility will rejoice when their record is opened.
- The one who lived in arrogance, heedlessness, or hypocrisy will be overcome with regret and terror.

So let each of us prepare—today—for the moment when every step, every word, and every intention will stand as testimony.

> *"That Day, mankind will proceed in scattered groups to be shown their deeds."*
> (Qur'an, Az-Zalzalah 99:6)

Let our deeds be the preparation for mercy,
and let our hearts be ready to meet the One whose justice is perfect and

whose mercy is boundless.

The Full Presentation of Deeds

Introduction

On the Day of Judgment, following resurrection and gathering, every human being will stand before God for the most revealing moment of their existence: the full presentation of deeds.

Nothing remains hidden.

Nothing is overlooked.

All that was said, done, intended, or concealed is unveiled in absolute clarity before divine justice.

Allah says:

> *"And the record [of deeds] will be placed, and you will see the criminals fearful of what is within it, and they will say, 'Woe to us! What is this book that leaves nothing small or great except that it has enumerated it?'"*
>
> (Qur'an, Al-Kahf 18:49)

1. What It Means to Present All Deeds

The full presentation is not a general summary—it is an exhaustive display:

- Every word ever spoken,

- Every glance and gesture,
- Every whispered thought and hidden motive,
- Every private intention and public action.

All is recorded. All is returned. All is revealed.

2. How the Presentation Occurs

This moment unfolds with unmatched clarity and finality:

- The **book of deeds** is laid open—flawless in detail.
- The **limbs testify**: hands, feet, tongue, and even skin speak the truth.
- The **earth itself bears witness** to the footprints of every act.

Allah says:

> *"That Day, it will report its news—because your Lord will have inspired it."*
>   (Qur'an, Az-Zalzalah 99:4–5)

There is no argument to offer, no denial to make. The truth speaks on behalf of the doer.

3. The Experience of the Presentation

This unveiling is not only external—it strikes the heart:

- **The righteous** receive their record in their right hand, reading it with joy:

"Here, read my record!" (Qur'an, Al-Haqqah 69:19)

- **The wicked** receive it in their left hand or behind their backs, overcome with despair:

"Oh, I wish I had not been given my record!" (Qur'an, Al-Haqqah 69:25)

Intentions are also made clear. What once lay buried beneath good appearances will be seen for what it truly was.

4. The Moral Weight of This Scene

This is more than a legal process—it is a moment of spiritual reckoning:

- Those whose scales are heavy with sincere deeds will feel comfort and triumph.
- Those whose lives were marked by heedlessness or hypocrisy will taste regret deeper than words can describe.

"But as for him whose balance is light—his refuge will be an abyss." (Qur'an, Al-Qari'ah 101:8–9)

5. Living with Awareness of This Presentation

To believe in the full presentation of deeds is to live in constant inner vigilance:

- Watching one's speech,

- Purifying intentions,
- Correcting actions,
- Seeking forgiveness before the record is sealed.

Allah says:

> *"He knows the treachery of the eyes and what the hearts conceal."*
> (Qur'an, Ghafir 40:19)

Even a false smile, a selfish prayer, or a forgotten kindness—each will have its moment in the light of truth.

Conclusion

The full presentation of deeds is not merely a scene to be feared—it is a moment of absolute unveiling:

- Where justice is perfected,
- Where no word is wasted,
- And where every soul meets its true self.

Let the wise prepare for the day when the ink of life is read aloud—
when every breath is remembered,
and every intention is known.
Let every step be guided by the certainty:
"You shall see it."
"And you shall be shown it."
"And you shall answer for it."

Standards of Acceptance and Rejection

Introduction

On the Day of Judgment, salvation is not granted by luck, nor is punishment meted out arbitrarily. In the Islamic worldview, the final outcome is governed by precise divine standards—measured by truth, guided by revelation, and executed with absolute justice.

These standards expose the reality behind every deed and every claim to faith. Nothing escapes the divine scales—neither the outward action nor the inward intention.

> *"So whoever does an atom's weight of good will see it,*
> *And whoever does an atom's weight of evil will see it."*
> (Qur'an, Az-Zalzalah 99:7–8)

1. Sound Faith as the Foundation

The first and most essential standard is the soundness of one's belief.

- **True monotheism (Tawheed),**
- **Faith in the messengers,**
- **Belief in the unseen: the Hereafter, the angels, the scriptures, and divine decree—**

- form the foundation upon which all deeds are built.

> *"Whoever seeks a religion other than Islam, it will never be accepted from him."*
> (Qur'an, Āl 'Imrān 3:85)

Without this foundation, even the most impressive actions hold no eternal weight. Faith is the soil; without it, no deed can take root.

2. Sincerity: The Soul of the Deed

Yet belief alone is not enough. Every action must spring from a heart seeking God's face—not praise, prestige, or reward from people.

> *"Unquestionably, for Allah is the pure religion."*
> (Qur'an, Az-Zumar 39:3)

Deeds tainted with showing off (riyā') are stripped of their light and become a burden on the Day of Judgment.

The Prophet ﷺ said:

> "What I fear most for my nation is minor shirk: showing off."
> *(Narrated by Ahmad)*

3. Conformity to Prophetic Guidance

True sincerity must be coupled with obedience. God only accepts deeds that align with His revelation and the example of His Prophet ﷺ.

> "Whoever does an act that is not in accordance with our command, it will be rejected."
> *(Narrated by Muslim)*

Innovation, no matter how well-intentioned, is not a substitute for obedience. The deed must be sincere—and correct.

4. Not Just Quantity, But Quality

On that Day, it is not the size of the deed that matters, but the heart behind it.

A single, sincere act can outweigh a mountain of heedless effort. God looks not at form or wealth, but at the intentions within the chest.

The Prophet ﷺ said:

> "Indeed, God does not look at your appearance or your wealth,
> but He looks at your hearts and your deeds."
> *(Narrated by Muslim)*

5. The Open Door of Repentance

Even those who faltered have hope—because the gate of repentance remains open until the soul departs.

> *"Indeed, Allah loves those who repent and purify themselves."*
> (Qur'an, Al-Baqarah 2:222)

True repentance erases sins and may even turn past wrongs into good deeds through sincere remorse and renewal of faith.

Conclusion

The standards of divine acceptance are neither hidden nor harsh:

- **A heart anchored in true faith,**
- **A soul sincere in intention,**
- **Actions that follow the path of revelation,**

- **And a spirit that seeks forgiveness and strives for better.**

These are the lights that guide one safely through the darkness of the Final Hour.

So let each day be a preparation for that inevitable meeting—when books are opened, secrets are unveiled, and the soul stands before its Lord, carrying only what it truly meant and truly did.

> *"And your Lord is never unjust to anyone."*
> (Qur'an, Al-Kahf 18:49)

VI

Hell and Paradise — The Eternal Destiny

Hell and Paradise represent the final and eternal destiny of every human soul—one of ultimate misery or pure bliss. Hell is not arbitrary punishment but the just consequence of deliberate rejection of truth, with torment that encompasses not only the body but also the psychological and spiritual dimensions of suffering. In contrast, Paradise is the realm of eternal joy, where every form of deficiency is absent and the soul is fulfilled beyond imagination. The greatest reward in Paradise is not merely its delights, but the closeness to God—the supreme goal that gives meaning to every act of faith and devotion in this life.

The Final Abode of the Human Soul

Introduction

After the scenes of resurrection, judgment, the Scale, and the full unveiling of deeds,
  humanity arrives at its most decisive moment:
  the determination of eternal destiny.
  This is not a symbolic conclusion—
  it is the final and permanent outcome of every choice made in life.
  There are only two eternal homes—no third:

- Paradise: the abode of peace, nearness to God, and everlasting joy.
- Hell: the realm of divine justice, separation from mercy, and lasting torment.

Allah says:

> "A group will be in Paradise, and a group will be in the Blaze."
> (Qur'an, Ash-Shura 42:7)

1. The Centrality of Eternal Destiny

This moment is the culmination of every step in the human journey:

- It manifests God's perfect justice and complete knowledge.
- It reflects the accumulated weight of belief, intention, and action.
- It seals the path each person chose—freely and fully—during their brief life.

There is no revision after this verdict, and no return.

2. Hell — The Realm of Everlasting Deprivation

Hell is the final destination for those who chose disbelief, hypocrisy, or persistent defiance without repentance.

- It is a place of physical, emotional, and spiritual torment.
- Its punishments are measured—just and appropriate to the severity of deeds.

Allah says:

> "And what can make you know what Saqar is?
> It lets nothing remain and leaves nothing [unburned]."
> (Qur'an, Al-Muddathir 74:27–28)

But Hell is not merely fire—it is the consequence of turning away from truth after it was made clear.
It is alienation from God after repeated invitations to draw near.

3. Paradise — The Abode of Eternal Bliss

Paradise is the reward of those who believed, strived, and remained sincere despite their flaws.

- It is a realm beyond imagination—no eye has seen, no ear has heard, and no heart has conceived.
- There is no fatigue, fear, or sadness within it.
- Its greatest gift is the eternal nearness to God and the vision of His noble Face.

Allah says:

> "Indeed, the righteous will be in gardens and bliss."
> (Qur'an, At-Tur 52:17)

Those who enter Paradise will forget every hardship of the world and dwell in joy that never fades.

4. The Finality of Destiny

- Once a soul enters Paradise or Hell, the decree is fixed.
- Disbelievers remain in Hell eternally—justice is served.
- As for sinful believers, God may pardon them by His mercy or accept intercession on their behalf.

Allah says:

> "Abiding therein forever."
> (Qur'an, At-Tawbah 9:100)

There is no appeal.
  No second life.

Only what was sown in this world can be harvested in the next.

The Central Message of This Section

This is the conclusion of the human journey—
　not into nonexistence,
　but into an eternal reality crafted by the very choices we made in freedom and full awareness.
　Eternity reveals the true weight of life's briefest moments.

A Call for Reflection

While the heart still beats and the sun still rises, the path remains open.
　The gates of repentance have not closed.
　The mercy of God is vast.
　Even one sincere step today can shift the weight of eternity.
　Let every soul pause and ask:
　Which path am I walking?
　What destination am I truly preparing for?

Hell — The Abode of Eternal Misery

Introduction

In the Islamic worldview, Hell (Jahannam) is not a metaphor, nor a symbolic concept meant to frighten the imagination. It is a real, created realm — a domain of ultimate consequence. It is the final destination for those who knowingly rejected divine guidance, choosing arrogance over humility, corruption over righteousness, and disbelief over faith.

Allah says:

"And fear the Fire which has been prepared for the disbelievers."
(Qur'an, Āl 'Imrān 3:131)

Hell is the arena where three forms of suffering converge:

- Physical torment,
- Psychological anguish,
- And spiritual estrangement from the mercy of God.

1. Descriptions of Hell in Revelation

The Qur'an and the Sunnah offer vivid and terrifying portrayals of Hell, not to instill despair, but to awaken hearts and redirect heedless souls.

Its Heat:

- The fire of Hell is beyond imagination. The Prophet ﷺ said:

    "Your fire is one part of seventy parts of the fire of Hell."
    (*Agreed upon*)

Its Gates:

- It has **seven gates**, each assigned to a specific class of sinner.

    "It has seven gates; for every gate is of them a portion designated."
    (Qur'an, Al-Ḥijr 15:44)

Its Depth and Darkness:

- The pit of Hell is unfathomably deep. Its darkness is pierced only by the flames of punishment, not by light or hope.

Chains and Shackles:

- Its inhabitants are bound, restrained, and humiliated.

    "Indeed, We have prepared for the disbelievers chains and shackles and a blaze."
    (Qur'an, Al-Insān 76:4)

2. The Inhabitants of Hell

Hell is not indiscriminate. Its punishments are tailored to the nature and severity of people's crimes:

- **Disbelievers:** Those who denied God, His messengers, and the Afterlife.
- **Hypocrites:** Those who outwardly professed faith but concealed denial and mockery.
- **Tyrants and the corrupt:** Those who spread injustice and oppressed others.
- **Sinful believers:** Those who committed major sins without repenting — though they may still receive divine forgiveness or intercession.

Degrees of Punishment:

Hell has levels. Its torment increases according to the depth of rejection, hypocrisy, or sin. The worst punishment is for those who consciously led others astray after rejecting the truth.

3. The Punishments Within Hell

Hell's torments are layered — each more severe than the last — designed not only to inflict pain but to expose the reality of the soul's rebellion.

Boiling drink:

- Liquids that sear the throat and disintegrate the insides.

Zaqqum Tree:

- A cursed tree at the pit of Hell. Its fruits are like heads of devils, and when eaten, burn from within.

"Its fruits will boil in their bellies like scalding water."
　(Qur'an, Ad-Dukhān 44:46)

Burning and Skin Replacement:

"Every time their skins are roasted, We will replace them with other skins so they may taste the punishment."
　(Qur'an, An-Nisā' 4:56)

Psychological Torment:

- The people of Hell beg to return, to die, to be forgotten. But none of these are granted.

4. The Greatest Loss: Separation from God

Amidst all the pain, the most unbearable punishment is **being veiled from the Face of God**.

"No! Surely, they will be veiled from their Lord that Day."
　(Qur'an, Al-Muṭaffifīn 83:15)

This spiritual estrangement — the total absence of divine mercy and nearness — is the most profound agony of all. In Hell, joy, hope, and light are extinguished — not only from the environment, but from within the soul itself.

5. The Purpose of Describing Hell

The mention of Hell in Islamic revelation is not to foster despair, but to:

- Shake the complacent,
- Awaken the heedless,
- Encourage repentance,
- And fortify the believer's resolve.

The Prophet ﷺ said:

> "If you knew what I know, you would laugh little and weep much."
> (*Agreed upon*)

Hell is not the destination God desires for His servants. He warns of it so that they may be saved from it.

Conclusion

Hell is the final destination for those who, with knowledge and clarity, turned their backs on God's mercy and chose rebellion.

Yet its very existence is a testimony to divine justice:

- No punishment without cause.
- No one wronged.
- No one cast into Hell without the full weight of truth against them.

Whoever reflects on the reality of Hell will not delay in returning to God.

- They will purify their heart.
- They will strive in righteous deeds.
- They will seek the shade of divine mercy before the fire closes in.

"And Allah invites to the Home of Peace and guides whom He wills to a straight path."
(Qur'an, Yūnus 10:25)

Why Divine Punishment Is Just: The Ethics of Hell

Introduction

In the Islamic worldview, divine punishment—especially the reality of Hell—is not an act of blind vengeance or arbitrary cruelty. Rather, it is a manifestation of divine justice, rooted in God's perfect wisdom, knowledge, and mercy.

Punishment in the Hereafter is not imposed without reason. It corresponds precisely to the moral weight of human choices made in full awareness and freedom. As Allah affirms:

> **"And your Lord is not ever unjust to the servants."**
> (Qur'an, *Fussilat* 41:46)

1. Punishment as a Requirement of Justice

Justice demands distinction: between the one who believes and the one who denies, between the one who reforms and the one who corrupts. If the oppressor and the oppressed, the sincere and the hypocrite, were treated equally—justice would be meaningless.

195

"[Hellfire is] a fitting recompense!"
(Qur'an, *An-Naba* 78:26)

Thus, those who knowingly reject guidance and actively spread corruption are not victims of fate—they are recipients of justice based on what they deliberately chose.

2. Punishment Upholds Moral Responsibility

God has given human beings intellect, moral intuition, and the freedom to choose. He clarified right and wrong and revealed the consequences of both. Each soul is tested within the scope of its capacity.

"Indeed, We guided him to the way—be he grateful or ungrateful."
(Qur'an, *Al-Insan* 76:3)

Without accountability, freedom loses its moral meaning. Divine punishment is not a violation of mercy—it is a necessary expression of truth and fairness.

3. The Proportionality of Punishment

Punishment in the Hereafter is not uniform. It is measured—scaled according to the degree of transgression, persistence in wrongdoing, and the impact of one's evil.

"And for all are degrees according to what they have done."
(Qur'an, *Al-An'am* 6:132)

• The most intense punishments are for those who denied God, mocked

His signs, and committed great injustices.

- Lesser punishments may befall those who sinned without arrogance but failed to repent.

This graded system reflects the absolute precision of divine justice.

4. Hell as the Natural Outcome of Human Choices

God does not force people into Hell. He invites them to truth, offers signs, grants time—and leaves the door of repentance wide open. But some choose another path.

> **"So taste [the punishment] for what you forgot of the meeting of this Day of yours."**
> (Qur'an, *As-Sajdah* 32:14)

Hell is not a trap. It is the end point of a road traveled knowingly. Just as fire burns regardless of one's regrets, so do spiritual consequences manifest from one's free decisions.

5. Mercy Amidst Justice

Even within the framework of divine punishment, God's mercy shines through:

- Some sinful believers are forgiven outright.
- Others are purified through temporary punishment, then granted Paradise.
- Intercession, repentance, and good deeds may erase or lessen one's burden.

> **"Why would Allah punish you if you are grateful and believe?"**
> (Qur'an, *An-Nisa* 4:147)

No one is punished without full warning, and no one is beyond the reach of God's mercy—except those who freely choose to reject it.

Conclusion

The punishment of Hell is not a divine cruelty—it is the inevitable consequence of rejecting truth and abusing the gift of freedom. It reflects a moral order in which every soul is honored with agency and judged by the standard of truth.

- No one is wronged.
- No burden is misplaced.
- No injustice occurs.

The wise reflect on this not to despair, but to awaken. The door to salvation remains open—for those who seek truth, purify intention, and walk the path of righteousness before the day when justice alone will speak.

> **"Whoever fears the standing before his Lord and restrains the soul from desires, then indeed, Paradise will be his refuge."**
> (Qur'an, *An-Nazi'at* 79:40–41)

The Torment of Hell: Its Psychological and Spiritual Dimensions

Introduction

In the Islamic worldview, the torment of Hell is not limited to physical suffering. Rather, it is a **comprehensive punishment** that strikes at the **core of human existence**—affecting the **body, mind, and soul**. It is not merely the burning of flesh but the extinguishing of hope, peace, and nearness to God.

Allah says:

> *"So taste! And We will not increase you except in punishment."*
> (Qur'an, An-Naba 78:30)

This is the **full weight of Hell's misery**—a torment beyond imagination.

1. Physical Torment

The bodily punishments in Hell are terrifying:

- **Unbearable heat** that far exceeds earthly fire.
- **Food** from the cursed tree of *Zaqqum*, bitter and boiling in the belly.
- **Drink** of scalding *Hamim*, tearing through the insides.

- **Chains and shackles**, binding the condemned in torment.

Allah says:

> *"They will have canopies of fire above them and canopies below them."*
> (Qur'an, Az-Zumar 39:16)

But this physical pain is only the outermost layer of a deeper agony.

2. Psychological Torment

As the fire scorches their bodies, a deeper fire rages within the souls of Hell's inhabitants:

Crushing Regret:

- They beg to return to the world—just to do one righteous deed. But the door is sealed.

> *"Our Lord! Bring us out, we will do righteousness—not what we used to do."*
> (Qur'an, Fatir 35:37)

Despair without End:

- All hope of relief is erased. They are told: *"Remain in it forever."*

Isolation and Betrayal:

- False leaders and companions who misled them are nowhere to be found.

"Now we have no intercessors, nor any close friend."
(Qur'an, Ash-Shu'ara 26:100–101)

This psychological torment is **a fire within the conscience**—a punishment that memory itself cannot escape.

3. Spiritual Torment

The **deepest pain** of all lies in **spiritual loss**:

Veiling from God:

- The people of Hell are **cut off from the vision of God's noble face**—the greatest joy in Paradise.

"No! Surely they will be veiled from [seeing] their Lord that Day."
(Qur'an, Al-Mutaffifin 83:15)

Exclusion from Mercy:

- They are cast far from divine grace, abandoned to their fate.

> *"Indeed, whoever comes to his Lord as a criminal—for him is Hell. He will neither die therein nor live."*
>   (Qur'an, Ta-Ha 20:74)

Gnawing Guilt:

- The soul fully comprehends that this torment is self-inflicted—that every moment of neglect led here.

4. The Full Weight of Hell's Misery

Hell is not merely fire. It is:

- The **screaming of the body**,
- The **shattering of the mind**,
- The **starvation of the soul**.

This trinity of torment makes Hell a realm of **total collapse**—where no part of the human being remains untouched by suffering.

5. Justice and Mercy in Hell's Reality

Despite its horror, the torment of Hell is **not blind cruelty**—it is **justice**:

- God only punishes those upon whom proof has been established.
- No one is wronged, and every soul reaps what it chose.

And **God's mercy** still surrounds this truth:

- **He sent messengers** and scriptures to warn.
- **He forgives those who turn to Him**, no matter their past.

- **No punishment comes without prior warning**.

Allah says:

> *"We would not punish [a people] until We had sent a messenger."*
> (Qur'an, Al-Isra 17:15)

Conclusion

The torment of Hell is **not just about pain**—it is about **isolation, loss, and rejection of what is most true and beautiful**.

Whoever contemplates this reality with sincerity will be moved to repentance, devotion, and spiritual clarity.

Let each heart ask:

Am I walking toward the Fire—or fleeing from it?

Paradise — The Abode of Pure Bliss

Introduction

After a life of faith, struggle, and striving, the believer arrives at the gate of eternal joy: **Paradise**—the supreme fulfillment of hope, the final destination of the righteous, and the highest expression of divine mercy.

Paradise is not an incidental reward or a distant wish.

It is the fruit of God's grace and justice,

and the crowning result of a life lived with sincerity, patience, and love for the Divine.

Allah says:

> *"But those who feared their Lord will be driven in groups to Paradise..."*
> **(Qur'an, Az-Zumar 39:73)**

1. The Nature of Paradise

Paradise is a realm where sorrow cannot enter and joy never departs.

- There is no illness, no fatigue, no fear, no regret.
- The believer lives in everlasting peace and delight—both physical and spiritual.

The Prophet 鸞 said:

> "In it are things no eye has seen, no ear has heard, and no human heart has ever imagined."
>   (Agreed upon: Bukhari & Muslim)

It is a world beyond comprehension, where longing is fulfilled before it is even voiced.

2. Descriptions of Paradise

a) Palaces and Rivers

Gardens of unimaginable beauty stretch as far as the soul can see.
    Palaces shimmer with gold, silver, and pearls.
    Rivers of fresh water, sweet milk, fragrant wine, and pure honey flow endlessly beneath them.

> *"In it are rivers of water unaltered, milk whose taste never changes..."*
>   **(Qur'an, Muhammad 47:15)**

b) Food and Drink

Fruits descend at the mere wish of the believer.
    No toil. No scarcity. Only abundance.

c) Pure Companions

Spouses are purified from all harm, united in eternal peace, love, and delight.

d) Eternal Life

There is no death in Paradise.
  The joy is continuous. The blessings never diminish.

3. The Spiritual Joys of Paradise

More profound than the gardens and rivers is the **nearness to God**—the soul's deepest desire.

a) God's Pleasure

The believer feels God's pleasure forever, a joy surpassing all other joys.

> *"And the pleasure of Allah is greater."*
>   **(Qur'an, At-Tawbah 9:72)**

b) The Vision of God

The ultimate gift: to behold the Face of the Lord without veil.
  The Prophet ﷺ said:

> "Indeed, you will see your Lord as clearly as you see the full moon—without any difficulty."
>   (Agreed upon)

In that moment, all the delights of Paradise pale beside the radiance of the Divine Face—
  a sight that makes every earthly trial worth enduring.

4. The Ranks of Paradise's Inhabitants

Paradise has degrees and stations, each reflecting the purity of one's faith and the weight of one's deeds.

- The highest ranks are for the prophets, the truthful, the martyrs, and the righteous.
- Others follow in beauty and order, according to their striving.

"So let the competitors compete [for this]."
(Qur'an, Al-Mutaffifin 83:26)

5. The Path to Paradise

Paradise is not gained by wishing, but by walking the path:

- **Faith**: sincere belief in God, His messengers, and the unseen.
- **Righteous action**: worship, justice, charity, and humility.
- **Patience**: in hardship, in obedience, and in resisting temptation.

"And race toward forgiveness from your Lord and a Paradise as wide as the heavens and the earth."
(Qur'an, Aal-'Imran 3:133)

Conclusion:

Paradise is the eternal homeland of the soul,
where peace is perfect, joy is limitless, and the heart finally rests.
It is:

- A joy without sadness,
- A home without loss,
- A nearness to God unbarred by any veil.

So let us strive.

Let every breath bring us closer.

Let every deed call us forward.

Let every longing anchor us to the hope of the Gardens.

Because Paradise is for those who prepare for it,

and the gates of eternity await those who walk toward them with sincerity.

The Nature of Eternal Bliss

Introduction

The bliss that God has promised the inhabitants of Paradise is not a fleeting comfort or worldly indulgence.

It is a complete, everlasting joy that encompasses every dimension of human existence— **body, mind, and soul**—without flaw, fatigue, or end. Allah says:

> "Indeed, the righteous will be in gardens and pleasure."
> (Qur'an, At-Tur 52:17)

1. True Eternity

The joy of Paradise is not touched by death, decay, or disruption.

There is no illness to weaken the body, no aging to fade beauty, no sadness to burden the heart.

Allah declares:

> "They will abide therein forever."
> (Qur'an, An-Nisa 4:57)

Here, **eternity magnifies joy**—for what could be more satisfying than delight that never fades, and peace that never ends?

2. Complete Physical Delight

The senses will awaken to pleasures unknown in the worldly realm:

- Food more delicious than the finest cuisines of Earth.
- Drinks that refresh without intoxication or impurity.
- Palaces adorned with gold, silver, and radiant pearls.
- Rivers flowing effortlessly through shaded gardens of splendor.

The Prophet ﷺ said:

> "In it are things no eye has seen, no ear has heard, and no human heart has ever imagined."
> *(Agreed upon)*

In Paradise, desire is not restrained—it is fulfilled in the most noble, elevated form.

3. Absolute Psychological Happiness

The soul finds perfect rest.
There is no grief from the past, no fear of the future.
Only serenity, security, and radiant joy.
Allah says:

> *"There will be no fear concerning them, nor will they grieve."*
> (Qur'an, Yunus 10:62)

All the pain endured in this world—loss, betrayal, isolation—is not only erased but reversed.
Families are reunited, hearts are healed, and laughter returns to the

tongue without sorrow behind it.

4. Spiritual Elevation

Beyond the gardens, rivers, and comforts, there lies the highest reward: **the pleasure of God** and the honor of beholding His noble face.

> *"And the pleasure of Allah is greater."*
> (Qur'an, At-Tawbah 9:72)

The Prophet ﷺ said:

> "Indeed, you will see your Lord as clearly as you see the full moon."
> *(Agreed upon)*

This vision—free of pain, separation, or distance—surpasses every other joy.

For the believer, it is not Paradise alone that fulfills the soul—but nearness to the One who created it.

5. Paradise vs. Worldly Pleasures

Worldly pleasure is always incomplete:

- It comes with fatigue.
- It fades with time.
- It is followed by regret, anxiety, or emptiness.

But in Paradise, **joy is pure**—untainted by loss, unspoiled by grief.

The Prophet ﷺ said:

> "The space of a whip in Paradise is better than the whole world and everything in it."

(Agreed upon)

What is fleeting here is surpassed by what is everlasting there.

Conclusion:

The nature of eternal bliss in Paradise is not merely luxury—it is **perfection in every form**:

- A peace that no sorrow can touch,
- A joy that no time can erode,
- A closeness to God that no veil can separate.

Paradise is the truest home of the human soul—
a destination for the sincere,
a reward for the patient,
and a longing that only faith and righteous action can fulfill.
So ask yourself:
What are you doing to walk toward that eternal joy?

Closeness to God — The Ultimate Goal

Introduction

In the Islamic view of the Hereafter, the pleasures of Paradise are not limited to rivers of milk, gardens of delight, or palaces of gold. These are immense blessings—but the supreme joy, the truest reward, is something far greater:

Closeness to God, the Almighty.

This nearness is the summit of eternal bliss, the longing that has stirred the hearts of prophets, saints, and sincere believers since the beginning of time. Allah says:

> "Indeed, the righteous will be among gardens and rivers,
> in a seat of honor near a Sovereign, Perfect in Ability."
> (Qur'an, Al-Qamar 54–55)

1. The Meaning of Closeness to God

This nearness is not spatial or physical. God is beyond time and space. Rather, it is the nearness of:

- **Witnessing** divine majesty,

213

- **Dwelling in** God's favor,
- **Basking in** His love and eternal approval,
- And, ultimately, **beholding His Noble Face** without veil.

It is a nearness that overwhelms the heart with tranquility and fills the soul with a joy no worldly bliss can imitate.

Allah says:

> "Faces, that Day, will be radiant—looking at their Lord."
> *(Qur'an, Al-Qiyamah 75:22–23)*

2. The Greatest Joy of Paradise

All the delights of Paradise pale in comparison to this singular moment:
The vision of God.

The Prophet ﷺ said:

> *"Indeed, you will see your Lord just as you see the full moon—clearly and without difficulty."*
> (Agreed upon)

This is not simply seeing with the eyes—this is a meeting of the soul with its Source, a communion beyond words.

Those who attain it will forget every pain, every hardship, every sacrifice they endured in the world.

3. Ranks of Closeness Based on Deeds

Not all in Paradise experience this nearness equally. The degrees of closeness depend on:

- The depth of **faith,**

- The purity of **intention,**
- The intensity of **love for God,**
- And the consistency of **obedience and devotion.**

Allah says:

> "And if he is of those brought near [to Allah]…"
> *(Qur'an, Al-Waqi'ah 56:88)*

These elite—**the Muqarrabūn**—are the spiritual nobility of the Hereafter. Their nearness is not a privilege—it is the fruit of hearts refined through patience, sincerity, and longing.

4. Divine Nearness and Inner Peace

Closeness to God is not only about reward—**it is the soul's true rest.**

- No more distance.
- No more longing.
- Only the serenity of being fully known, fully accepted, fully loved.

Allah says:

> "Allah is pleased with them, and they are pleased with Him."
> *(Qur'an, Al-Ma'idah 5:119)*

This is not a joy that fades, nor a moment that passes. It is **eternal contentment**—as boundless as the mercy that grants it.

5. The Path to Closeness Begins Here

To draw near to God in the Hereafter, we must first draw near to Him here:

- Through **sincere faith,**
- Through **acts done purely for His sake,**
- Through **frequent remembrance (dhikr),**
- Through **repentance** that purifies the heart,
- And through **a love for God** that surpasses all else.

In a divine hadith (Hadith Qudsi), God says:

> *"My servant continues to draw near to Me through supererogatory acts until I love him..."*
>   (Reported by Bukhari)

Each act of sincerity, each whispered prayer, each moment of turning back to God—**it all counts.**

Conclusion:

Closeness to God is the true Paradise. It is the greatest reward, the highest joy, the culmination of the soul's journey.

- A joy untainted by fear,
- A nearness unmarred by separation,
- A vision that never dims.

Whoever yearns for this meeting must strive now—with a heart alive in remembrance, and a soul reaching upward in every deed.

For those who walk the path of nearness today, **the gates of eternal intimacy will open tomorrow**.

VII

The Complete Structure of Religion — Islam, Faith, and Excellence (Iḥsān)

The complete structure of religion in Islam is built upon three interwoven dimensions: Islam (submission), Imān (faith), and Iḥsān (spiritual excellence). The Pillars of Islam form the practical framework through acts of worship like prayer, fasting, charity, and pilgrimage. The Pillars of Faith outline the doctrinal foundation, including belief in God, angels, divine books, prophets, the Last Day, and divine decree. At the peak stands Iḥsān—worshiping Allah as though one sees Him—which transforms religious practice into a conscious, heartfelt journey. Together, these three levels shape a complete human being whose life is rooted in belief, guided by action, and elevated through inner awareness.

Islam, Faith, and Excellence

Introduction

After tracing the human journey from creation to resurrection, and from trial to eternal destiny, we must return to the foundation upon which this entire path is built:

the complete structure of religion.

This divine framework—revealed to guide, elevate, and save—is composed of three interwoven levels:

- **Islam**: the outward practice of worship and obedience,
- **Faith (Imān)**: the inward certainty and belief that roots the soul,
- **Excellence (Iḥsān)**: the highest refinement of awareness and sincerity before God.

As the Prophet Muhammad ﷺ taught in the renowned Hadith of Jibrīl:

> "That you worship God as though you see Him; and if you do not
> see Him, then know that He sees you."
> *(Reported by Bukhārī and Muslim)*

1. Religion as a Comprehensive Way of Life

In the Islamic worldview, religion is not a compartment of life, nor a set of abstract doctrines.

It is a **total vision of existence**—one that defines truth, shapes behavior, and gives meaning to every action.

It is:

- A framework for navigating moral and spiritual reality,
- A compass guiding the heart toward what is right,
- A path that links the temporary world with eternal consequence.

Allah says:

> "Indeed, the religion in the sight of Allah is Islam."
> (Qur'an, Āl 'Imrān 3:19)

2. The Three Pillars: Islam, Faith, and Excellence

Each of these three dimensions builds upon the other—forming a unified structure:

a) Islam – The Foundation of Obedience

The outward expression of submission to God through action:

- Testifying to the Oneness of God and the prophethood of Muhammad ﷺ,
- Performing the five daily prayers,
- Giving charity, fasting in Ramadan, and making pilgrimage to Mecca.

Islam is the **gateway** through which the servant begins their journey toward their Lord.

b) Faith (Imān) – The Anchor of Belief

True religion cannot stand without inner belief.

Imān is certainty in the unseen: belief in God, the angels, the divine books, the messengers, the Last Day, and divine decree.

It is the **engine of conviction** that animates outward action.

c) Excellence (Iḥsān) – The Pinnacle of Sincerity

At its height, religion becomes more than action or belief—it becomes **presence**.

Iḥsān is to live in deep consciousness of God:

- To act as though seeing Him,
- To speak and move knowing He sees you.

This is the **spiritual summit** of the human journey.

3. The Interdependence of the Three Levels

Each pillar strengthens the others:

- Without Islam, belief lacks structure.
- Without Imān, deeds are hollow and lifeless.
- Without Iḥsān, worship loses its beauty and sincerity.

The Prophet ﷺ presented all three together—not as options, but as **components of a single living religion**.

4. The Path of Salvation through the Structure of Religion

This triad is the **only path** to eternal salvation.

It aligns the soul with divine truth, and prepares the human being to meet their Lord with a heart of light.

Allah says:

> *"And whoever submits his face to Allah while being a doer of good—he has grasped the firmest handhold."*
> (Qur'an, Luqmān 31:22)

Conclusion

The complete structure of religion—**Islam, Faith, and Excellence**—is not a ladder of superiority, but a **symphony of wholeness**.

Through sincere belief, righteous action, and constant remembrance of God, the soul becomes whole—and the journey toward eternal joy begins.

This is the map drawn by divine mercy,

the path walked by the prophets and the righteous,

and the road that leads to the greatest reward:

Closeness to God and His eternal pleasure.

The Pillars of Islam — The Practical Structure

Introduction

Islam is not merely a belief held in the heart—it is a living, practiced faith that shapes every aspect of human life. At the center of this dynamic system stand the five pillars: the foundational acts that translate faith into action, belief into behavior, and intention into transformation.

The Prophet Muhammad ﷺ said:

> *"Islam is built upon five..."*
> *(Agreed upon by Bukhārī and Muslim)*

These five are not arbitrary duties; they are the divine architecture of a life anchored in servitude to God.

1. The Practical Framework of Religion

Islam is a religion of movement and manifestation. Its teachings are not confined to texts or temples, but woven into the fabric of daily life.

- True belief is incomplete without practice.
- The five pillars offer a daily, seasonal, and lifetime rhythm that sustains

the believer's journey.

- They guide the heart, discipline the body, and shape the soul's relationship with God, self, and society.

Allah says:

> "And who is better in religion than one who submits his face to Allah while being a doer of good?"
> (Qur'an, Al-Nisā' 4:125)

2. The Five Pillars of Islam

Each pillar is a divine command and a spiritual opportunity.

1. The Shahādah (Declaration of Faith)

"To bear witness that there is no god but Allah, and Muhammad is His Messenger."

- This is the soul's awakening—the entry into divine covenant.
- It affirms God's exclusive right to worship and the commitment to follow His final Prophet ﷺ.

2. Prayer (Ṣalāh)

Five daily connections with the Creator, spaced throughout the day.

- Prayer is the rhythm of remembrance, a divine meeting that renews the heart's orientation.
- The Prophet ﷺ said:

> *"Prayer is light."*

(Reported by Muslim)

3. Charity (Zakāh)

An act of purification—of wealth and the heart.

- Zakāh restores economic balance and expresses compassion through tangible support.
- It reminds the believer that all provision is from God, and meant to be shared.

4. Fasting in Ramadan (Ṣawm)

A month of spiritual training through abstinence.

- Fasting tempers desire, teaches patience, and draws the soul nearer to its Creator.
- It is hunger with a purpose, silence with meaning.

5. The Pilgrimage (Ḥajj)

A journey of body and spirit to the sacred heart of Islam.

- Hajj is the embodiment of humility and submission.
- It is the believer's rehearsal for the Day of Judgment—stripped of titles, immersed in unity.

3. Wisdom in the Divine Sequence

The order of the pillars mirrors the journey of the soul:

- **Shahādah** roots the heart in truth.
- **Prayer** trains the self in daily devotion.

- **Zakāh** instills generosity and social responsibility.
- **Fasting** disciplines the inner self.
- **Ḥajj** completes the circle in a climactic act of surrender.

Together, they construct the full edifice of spiritual integrity.

4. The Transformational Power of the Pillars

Living the pillars faithfully:

- **Instills core virtues** like sincerity, resilience, and compassion.
- **Purifies the soul**, steadily cultivating God-consciousness (taqwā).
- **Builds a just society** where wealth circulates, hearts soften, and unity is practiced.

Each pillar is a brick in the bridge between this life and the next.
  Allah says:

> "He has certainly succeeded who purifies himself, and mentions the name of his Lord and prays."
> (Qur'an, Al-Aʿlā 87:14–15)

Conclusion

The five pillars of Islam are not just religious rituals—they are divine instruments that shape a holistic, purposeful life. They link belief with behavior, and elevate everyday acts into acts of worship.

Whoever walks these five paths with sincerity and steadfastness:

- Builds a life of meaning,
- Anchors their soul in divine nearness,
- And travels the straight road toward Paradise.

Let each believer uphold these pillars not merely out of obligation, but with love, reverence, and the certainty that they are building—stone by stone—their eternal home.

Detailed Explanation of the Five Pillars of Islam

Introduction

Islam, at its heart, is not confined to belief held in the mind or heart alone.

It is a living, breathing system of practice that organizes a person's entire relationship—with God, the self, and society.

The Prophet Muhammad ﷺ encapsulated this practical framework in his famous words:

> *"Islam is built upon five..."*
> *(Agreed upon by Bukhārī and Muslim)*

These five pillars are not mere rituals; they are the foundation of the believer's life—daily, seasonal, and lifelong acts that transform faith into action and worship into a way of being.

1. The Concept of a Practical Structure in Religion

Islam is a religion that walks alongside the believer, guiding them through every stage of life.

- It begins in the heart, but expresses itself through the body.

- It does not ask for theoretical belief alone, but for active devotion that shapes character and community.

Through the five pillars, Islam provides a clear, tangible map for living in divine presence.

> *"And who is better in religion than one who submits his face to Allah while being a doer of good?"*
> (Qur'an, Al-Nisā' 4:125)

2. The Five Pillars of Islam

First: The Two Testimonies (Shahādah) — The Gate of Entry

The journey begins with a declaration—
A witness from the soul that reshapes one's entire worldview.

- **"There is no god but Allah"** affirms the Oneness of God in His Lordship, worship, and attributes.
- **"Muhammad is the Messenger of Allah"** commits the believer to the path of guidance and mercy revealed through the Prophet ﷺ.

This testimony is not simply uttered; it is lived.
It is the key that unlocks the heart and binds the soul to divine truth.

> "Whoever says: There is no god but Allah will enter Paradise."
> *(Reported by Bukhārī)*

Second: Prayer (Ṣalāh) — The Daily Anchor

From the moment the believer enters Islam, prayer becomes their spiritual rhythm—
  Five calls a day to pause, return, and reconnect with the Source of peace.

- Prayer purifies the heart from distraction,
- Strengthens the soul with light,
- And trains the body in discipline and presence.

  "The first thing a person will be held accountable for on the Day of Judgment is his prayer."
    (*Reported by al-Nasā'ī*)

  "Establish prayer. Verily, prayer prevents immorality and wrongdoing."
    (Qur'an, Al-'Ankabūt 29:45)

Third: Zakāh — The Purification of Wealth and Soul

Zakāh is more than charity; it is spiritual economics.

- It purifies the wealth of the giver and dignifies the receiver.
- It builds a society rooted in justice and mutual care.
- It frees the heart from greed and awakens empathy for those in need.

  "Take from their wealth a charity to purify and cleanse them through it."
    (Qur'an, Al-Tawbah 9:103)

Fourth: Fasting in Ramadan (Ṣawm) — The Refinement of Will

Once a year, the body is trained to pause its appetites so the soul may rise.

- Fasting fosters patience, self-control, and sincerity.
- It teaches us hunger, so we may learn compassion.
- It is a month-long invitation to realign our lives with God's will.

> *"O you who believe, fasting has been prescribed for you...so that you may become righteous."*
> (Qur'an, Al-Baqarah 2:183)

Fifth: Pilgrimage (Ḥajj) — The Journey of Total Surrender

For those able, the pilgrimage to the Sacred House is the summit of devotion.

- It is the believer's return to the origin of tawḥīd,
- A journey of humility, unity, and remembrance,
- A reenactment of prophetic footsteps that echoes across generations.

> *"Pilgrimage to the House is a duty owed to Allah by all people who can find a way to do so."*
> (Qur'an, Āl 'Imrān 3:97)

3. The Wisdom in the Order of the Pillars

Each pillar builds upon the one before it:

- The **Shahādah** plants the seed of faith,
- **Prayer** waters it with constancy,
- **Zakāh** shares its fruits with others,
- **Fasting** protects it with self-restraint,
- And **Ḥajj** crowns it with ultimate surrender.

Together, they construct the full spiritual architecture of the believer.

4. The Impact of Upholding the Pillars

Those who live by the five pillars do not merely perform religion—
   They embody it.

- They become compassionate in wealth,
- Steadfast in hardship,
- Present in devotion,
- And peaceful in soul.

> *"He has certainly succeeded who purifies himself, and mentions the name of his Lord and prays."*
>   (Qur'an, Al-Aʿlā 87:14–15)

Conclusion:

The Five Pillars of Islam are not just obligations.
   They are lifelines.
   They move the believer from word to deed, from belief to beauty, and

from the temporal to the eternal.

Whoever upholds them with sincerity stands on the firm foundation of divine favor—

Walking a path lit with prayer, softened by charity, strengthened by fasting, crowned by pilgrimage,

and all held together by the unshakable truth of God's Oneness and Prophetic guidance.

Let every day be a renewal of these pillars—

and every breath a step closer to the pleasure of Allah.

The Pillars of Faith — The Doctrinal Structure

Introduction

If the five pillars of Islam form the visible structure of religious life, then the pillars of *faith* (*īmān*) are its internal foundation—the beliefs that nourish, sustain, and give meaning to every act of devotion. They are the roots from which sincere worship grows, anchoring the soul in certainty and spiritual purpose.

As the Prophet ﷺ said in the famous ḥadīth of Jibrīl:

> *"That you believe in Allah, His angels, His books, His messengers, the Last Day, and that you believe in divine decree—both the good and the bad of it."*
>
> (Reported by Muslim)

1. The Meaning of Faith (Īmān)

Faith in Islam is not merely intellectual assent or emotional feeling.
Linguistically, *īmān* means affirmation and trust. Technically, it is defined as:

- Belief in the heart,

234

- Declaration on the tongue,
- Action through the limbs.

It is a holistic state that shapes how a person sees the world, makes decisions, and lives their life.

> "The believers are only those who believe in Allah and His Messenger, and then do not doubt."
> (Qur'an, Al-Ḥujurāt 49:15)

2. The Six Pillars of Faith

These six core beliefs constitute the complete doctrinal framework of Islam. They are not optional or symbolic—they are essential to true faith and the foundation for salvation.

1. Belief in Allah

- Faith in His existence, oneness, names, attributes, and perfect justice.
- Worshiping Him with trust, love, fear, and hope.
- To believe in God is to orient the heart toward its ultimate source and goal.

2. Belief in the Angels

- Created from light, angels are unseen beings tasked with executing God's will:
- Bringing revelation, recording deeds, guarding humanity, and praising God.

Their presence reminds the believer that the world is full of unseen forces of order and mercy.

3. Belief in the Divine Books

- Affirming all scriptures sent by God to His messengers:
- The Torah, Psalms, Gospel, and the Qur'an.
- The Qur'an is the final, preserved revelation—a living guidance until the end of time.

Just as the angels deliver God's command, His books deliver His wisdom.

4. Belief in the Messengers

- Faith in all prophets sent to humanity, including Noah, Abraham, Moses, Jesus, and finally, Muhammad ﷺ.

Each one conveyed the same central truth: to worship God alone. To believe in them is to honor the chain of divine guidance across history.

5. Belief in the Last Day

- Belief in death, the grave, resurrection, judgment, Heaven, and Hell.

Reflecting on this Day inspires humility, accountability, and a focused heart.

6. Belief in Divine Decree (Qadar)

- Belief that everything occurs by God's will and wisdom.

Though all unfolds under divine knowledge, humans remain responsible for their choices—free to act, yet always under the sovereign plan of the All-Knowing.

"Indeed, We guided him to the way, whether he be grateful or ungrateful."
(Qur'an, Al-Insān 76:3)

3. Faith as a Unified Structure

These six beliefs are inseparable. One cannot be denied without undermining the entire foundation of Islamic faith.

"Each one believes in Allah, His angels, His books, and His messengers..."
(Qur'an, Al-Baqarah 2:285)

They are not merely theological concepts—they are truths that reshape how one sees the world, how one loves, fears, hopes, and lives.

4. The Transformative Power of Faith

True faith is not static. It brings about:

- Inner peace and reliance upon God,
- Detachment from worldly delusion,
- Trust in God's mercy during hardship,
- Deep awareness of one's purpose and end.

"Those who believe and whose hearts find tranquility in the remembrance of Allah—truly, in the remembrance of Allah do hearts find rest."
(Qur'an, Ar-Ra'd 13:28)

Faith doesn't remove hardship, but it gives hardship meaning. It does not erase pain, but it purifies and elevates it.

Conclusion:

The pillars of faith are not only doctrines to memorize—they are truths to embody.

They give the believer clarity in confusion, purpose in distraction, and certainty in a world full of doubt.

Whoever plants these beliefs firmly in their heart walks the path of light— anchored in God, guided by revelation, and hopeful of the Hereafter.

Let faith not remain in the tongue alone,

but sink into the soul,

so that the heart finds peace,

the actions find meaning,

and the soul finds its way home.

Detailed Explanation of the Six Pillars of Faith

Introduction

Faith (*īmān*) in Islam is not merely a set of abstract beliefs. It is the **inner compass** that shapes every intention, action, and hope. While the pillars of Islam represent the **visible structure** of religion, the six pillars of faith are its **invisible roots**—anchoring the heart, nurturing the soul, and sustaining the journey toward God.

The Prophet ﷺ summarized them in the famous Hadith:

> *"That you believe in Allah, His angels, His books, His messengers, the Last Day, and in divine decree—its good and its evil."*
> (Reported by Muslim)

These pillars together form the complete worldview of a believer: a lens through which one sees life, death, and eternity.

1. Belief in Allah — The Source of All Light

At the heart of all faith is belief in Allah: the **One**, the **Ever-Living**, the **Merciful Master of all worlds**. This belief is not only affirming His existence but embracing His centrality in every aspect of life.

It includes:

- **His existence**: undeniable and evident in all creation.
- **His lordship**: that He alone creates, sustains, gives life and death.
- **His divinity**: that only He is worthy of worship—none else.
- **His names and attributes**: majestic, perfect, and beyond comparison.

"The Messenger has believed in what was revealed to him from his Lord, and so have the believers..."
(Qur'an, 2:285)

Reflection:

Do I live as though Allah sees every moment of my life, or as if He is absent from it?

2. Belief in the Angels — Constant Companions in the Unseen

Belief in the angels is to believe that the unseen world is just as real as the visible one.

- Angels are **pure beings of light** who serve God's will without error.
- Among their roles:
- **Jibrīl** – bearer of revelation,
- **Mīkā'īl** – responsible for rain and provision,
- **Isrāfīl** – who will blow the trumpet of Resurrection,
- **Malak al-Mawt** – the angel of death who escorts the soul.

"The angels glorify the praises of their Lord and seek forgiveness for those on earth."
　　(Qur'an, 42:5)

Reflection:

Do I remember that every word I utter is recorded by noble scribes beside me?

3. Belief in the Divine Books — Light in the Darkness

God's mercy to humanity includes sending scriptures to guide and illuminate.

- These books were revealed to various prophets, including:
- The **Torah** to Moses,
- The **Psalms** to David,
- The **Gospel** to Jesus,
- The **Qur'an** to Muhammad ﷺ — the final and preserved revelation.

"He has sent down to you the Book in truth, confirming what came before it..."
　　(Qur'an, 3:3)

The Qur'an is not just a book to be recited; it is a **manual for life** and the **speech of God** to the human heart.

Reflection:

How often do I treat the Qur'an as a living guide, not just a sacred text?

4. Belief in the Messengers — A Chain of Divine Mercy

Throughout history, God sent prophets to guide humanity out of darkness. They were chosen not for status, but for their sincerity, strength, and truthfulness.

- We believe in all of them:
- **Noah**, **Abraham**, **Moses**, **Jesus**, and **Muhammad** ﷺ, the seal of the prophets.

"We make no distinction between any of His messengers..."
  (Qur'an, 2:285)

To believe in them means to honor their message, follow their way, and defend their legacy.

Reflection:
Do I reflect the character of the Prophet I claim to follow?

5. Belief in the Last Day — The Awakening After Life

Faith is not complete without belief in the **Day of Resurrection**—the day when every soul will stand before its Creator.
This includes belief in:

- Death and the grave,
- Resurrection and the gathering,
- The Reckoning and the Scale,
- Paradise and Hell,
- And the eternal nature of the hereafter.

"Indeed, those who believe and do righteous deeds – for them are Gardens of Bliss."
(Qur'an, 31:8)

Reflection:

Do I prepare for the final meeting with God as carefully as I prepare for this world?

6. Belief in Divine Decree (Qadar) — Trusting the Wise Planner

Divine decree means that everything—whether good or painful—occurs by God's will, knowledge, and wisdom.

- God knows all things before they occur.
- He has recorded all that will happen.
- He wills what is best, even when hidden from us.

"Indeed, We have created everything according to a decree."
(Qur'an, 54:49)

But this belief does not cancel human will—rather, it **balances faith in God's plan** with personal **accountability**.

Reflection:

When things go wrong, do I still trust that God's plan is better than mine?

Conclusion: Walking the Path of Certainty

The six pillars of faith are not just theological concepts. They are the **beating heart** of a believer's identity—shaping how we think, how we feel, and how we act.

Whoever believes in them sincerely, seeks to live by them daily, and nurtures them with knowledge and reflection,
walks upon a path of light—
a path that leads not only to peace in this world,
but eternal nearness to the One we were created to return to.

> *"Those who believe, and whose hearts find peace in the remembrance of Allah—verily in the remembrance of Allah do hearts find peace."*
>   (Qur'an, 13:28)

Iḥsān — The Spiritual Pinnacle

Introduction

Once the outer pillars of Islam are firmly grounded,
and the inner truths of faith take root in the heart,
the believer is invited to ascend—
to the loftiest peak of the spiritual path: **Iḥsān**.
Iḥsān is the summit of the faith journey.
It is the realm where worship becomes intimacy,
where deeds are not merely performed,
but polished by presence and perfected by love.
The Prophet ﷺ described it simply yet profoundly:

> "Iḥsān is to worship Allah as though you see Him;
> and if you do not see Him, know that He sees you."
> (Bukhārī and Muslim)

1. What Is Iḥsān?

Linguistically, iḥsān means beauty, excellence, and mastery.
Spiritually, it means to **worship with full presence of heart**,
to act not from duty alone, but from deep awareness.
It is the art of turning every moment—mundane or majestic—
into a silent conversation with God.

245

If one cannot "see" Him, then one walks with the certainty
that **His gaze never departs**.

2. The Two Wings of Iḥsān: Witnessing and Vigilance

Just as a bird soars only when both wings move in harmony,
so the path of Iḥsān rises through two spiritual states:

Witnessing (Mushāhadah)

To worship as though beholding Him—
the heart is filled with awe,
and the soul is drawn to beauty and nearness.

Vigilance (Murāqabah)

To walk with the certainty that God is watching—
quiet, steady, and humble under His gaze.
Witnessing lifts the soul;
vigilance anchors it with sincerity and reverence.
Those who live between the two glide on the winds of grace.

3. How Iḥsān Transforms Character

The one who lives with Iḥsān...

- **Prays not to finish**, but to meet.
- **Acts not for praise**, but for presence.
- **Purifies the heart** from vanity, hypocrisy, and restlessness.
- **Elevates every deed**, infusing it with beauty and intention.
- **Becomes tranquil**, content with whatever God decrees.

"Indeed, Allah is with those who are mindful of Him and those who excel."
  (Qur'an, An-Naḥl 16:128)

4. Iḥsān in Every Domain of Life

Iḥsān is not reserved for the prayer mat.
  It must pour into every corner of the human experience:

- In **worship**: the body bows, but the heart is fully awake.
- In **transactions**: honesty, gentleness, and mercy shine.
- In **relationships**: forgiveness replaces vengeance.
- In **service**: sincerity eclipses show.
- In **speech and silence**: both become vessels of remembrance.

  "Indeed, Allah has prescribed excellence in all things."
  (Muslim)

5. Iḥsān — The Gateway to the Highest Paradise

The highest levels of Paradise are not reached
  by quantity of deeds alone,
  but by the **quality of the heart** behind them.
  The people of Iḥsān—those who loved God in secret and in hardship—
  are drawn closest to His Throne.

  "Is there any reward for excellence but excellence?"
  (Qur'an, Ar-Raḥmān 55:60)

Their reward is not only gardens and rivers,
  but the **pleasure of God**

and the **vision of His noble Face**.

Conclusion

Iḥsān is the soul of worship,
 the refinement of character,
 the fragrance of sincerity in the life of a believer.
 It is to live each moment in the shadow of God's gaze—
 until that shadow becomes a light within.
 So ask yourself:
 Do I worship as though I see Him?
 Or at least, do I live as though **He sees me**?
 Whoever lives by this awareness
 has already begun the journey into Paradise.

Worshiping Allah as Though You See Him

Introduction

Among the loftiest teachings imparted by the Prophet Muhammad ﷺ is that the ultimate purpose of worship is not mere outward performance, nor mechanical obedience to divine law. It is the ascent of the heart toward a state of spiritual witnessing—where the servant worships their Lord as though they behold Him with the eye of the soul.

The Prophet ﷺ said in the famous ḥadīth of Jibrīl:

> "Iḥsān is to worship Allah as though you see Him; and if you do not see Him, [know that] He sees you."
> *(Agreed upon – Bukhārī and Muslim)*

1. The Meaning of "As Though You See Him"

This profound phrase does not refer to physical sight in the worldly sense. Rather, it speaks of the heart's spiritual vision—a constant mindfulness of Allah's majesty and nearness:

- To feel, with the depth of one's soul, that Allah is before you.
- To let your heart tremble in reverence and overflow with love.

- To carry the awareness that every breath, step, and whisper is under His watchful gaze.

This is the worship of presence—not of habit, but of reverent intimacy. It transforms prayer into conversation, obedience into devotion, and life itself into a sanctuary of remembrance.

2. The Impact of This Station on the Worshiper

Whoever attains this level of worship:

- **Prays with awe**, as though standing before the Throne.
- **Acts with sincerity**, untouched by the desire for praise.
- **Walks the earth with humility**, aware of the Divine gaze.
- **Lets go of worldly attachments**, drawn by the sweetness of nearness to Allah.
- **Tastes tranquility**, born of constant awareness that they are never alone.

Allah says:

> *"Does he not know that Allah sees?"*
> (Qur'an, Al-'Alaq 96:14)

3. The Path to Reaching This Station

This station of spiritual witnessing is not attained by chance—it is reached by a heart that seeks and strives:

- **Sincere faith**, deeply rooted in knowledge of Allah's names and attributes.
- **Frequent remembrance**, by tongue and heart, until His name echoes

in one's soul.

- **Contemplation of His signs**, in the Qur'an and in creation.
- **Purification of intention**, doing all for His sake alone.
- **Love of Allah**, cultivated through obedience, gratitude, and du'ā.

Allah says:

> *"And keep yourself patient with those who call upon their Lord morning and evening, seeking His Face."*
> (Qur'an, Al-Kahf 18:28)

4. Worship Illuminated by Witnessing

This spiritual presence breathes life into all acts of worship:

- In **prayer**, the servant stands as if before Allah, listening and speaking with a heart wide open.
- In **fasting**, one abstains not just from food, but from every sin, in quiet devotion known only to the Lord.
- In **charity**, one gives with joy, knowing that what is hidden is more beloved to Allah.
- In **ḥajj**, the pilgrim walks not merely in sacred places, but in the shadow of God's majesty.

Every act becomes a moment of ascent—a step closer to the Divine.

5. The Fruit of This Worship in the Hereafter

Those who lived as though they saw Allah in this life will be granted the greatest reward in the next:

"Some faces on that Day will be radiant—looking at their Lord."
(Qur'an, Al-Qiyāmah 75:22–23)

The heart that once worshiped with unseen vision will be honored with **true vision**—the sight of Allah's noble Face, the highest delight in Paradise.

Conclusion

To worship Allah as though you see Him is the essence of Iḥsān, the pinnacle of faith, and the light that guides a soul to peace.

It is the path of those whose hearts are alive, whose deeds are sincere, and whose longing is for no place but near to Him.

Let each believer strive to rise:

- From routine to reverence,
- From form to essence,
- From worship seen by people to worship seen only by God.

For whoever walks this path in the shadows of the world will walk in light on the Day of Radiance.

Iḥsān as the Driving Force of the Complete Human Being

Introduction

In the comprehensive Islamic worldview, the human being is not viewed merely as a body or an intellect, but as a unified soul that brings together mind, faith, emotion, and conduct. Within this holistic vision, *iḥsān*—spiritual excellence—is the inner engine that drives the human being toward the fulfillment of their highest purpose: to worship Allah with beauty, sincerity, and presence.

As Allah says:

> *"Indeed, the most noble of you in the sight of Allah is the most righteous among you."*
> (Qur'an, Al-Ḥujurāt 49:13)

To live with *iḥsān* is to live with intention, integrity, and the constant awareness of the Divine gaze.

1. Iḥsān as a Catalyst for Excellence

Iḥsān propels the believer to rise above minimal obligations and pursue excellence in all aspects of worship and character. A *muḥsin*—a person of iḥsān—does not ask, "What is the least I must do?" but rather, "How can I do this with beauty and sincerity?"

This pursuit touches every act:

- Presence and humility in prayer,
- Purity and truth in fasting,
- Sincerity in charity,
- Devotion in da'wah,
- Compassion in daily dealings.

Iḥsān makes the soul ambitious—not for worldly status, but for spiritual refinement and closeness to God.

2. Iḥsān as a Blueprint for Wholeness

The muḥsin is not fragmented. Inwardly, they cultivate:

- Sincere intention,
- Awareness of Allah's gaze,
- Deep reverence and love.

Outwardly, they strive for:

- Justice in dealings,
- Gentleness in speech,
- Kindness in relationships.

As Allah commands:

> *"And do good; indeed, Allah loves the doers of good."*
> (Qur'an, Al-Baqarah 2:195)

This integration of heart and action shapes a human being who is spiritually balanced and ethically grounded.

3. Iḥsān and Ethical Leadership

The journey of iḥsān does not end with the self—it naturally radiates outward. The muḥsin becomes a moral light in their environment:

- They raise families on sincerity and mercy,
- Lead in workplaces with integrity,
- Serve communities with compassion and justice.

They live not to dominate, but to elevate. In this, they fulfill their divine role:

> *"Indeed, I will make upon the earth a successive authority [khalīfah]."*
> (Qur'an, Al-Baqarah 2:30)

4. Iḥsān and the Spirit of Generosity

The person of iḥsān gives not only what is required, but what is beautiful. They give:

- Time without resentment,
- Kindness without expectation,
- Wealth without pride.

Even a smile, a gesture of forgiveness, or a quiet prayer becomes a reflection of inner excellence.

> *"And they give food, in spite of love for it, to the needy, the orphan, and the captive."*
> (Qur'an, Al-Insān 76:8)

In this way, the muḥsin nourishes not just bodies, but hearts.

5. Iḥsān as the Peak of the Journey to God

Ultimately, iḥsān is the summit of spiritual ascent. It is not an accessory to religion, but its crown. It is the level of those who live *as though they see Allah*—and even when they do not, know with certainty that He sees them.
The Prophet ﷺ said:

> "Indeed, Allah has prescribed iḥsān in everything…"
> *(Reported by Muslim)*

These are the souls who will be closest to Allah in Paradise, honored by His pleasure, and invited to the most exalted nearness.

> *"Is there any reward for excellence except excellence?"*
> (Qur'an, Ar-Raḥmān 55:60)

Conclusion:

Iḥsān is not a final decorative layer—it is the essence of living fully, beautifully, and with complete awareness. It animates the heart, polishes character, and illuminates the path to Allah.
Whoever chooses iḥsān as their compass

- rises above ego and excess,
- uplifts others through grace,
- and walks with light in this life and the next.

These are the *awliyā'* of Allah—His close friends—*"upon whom there is no fear, nor shall they grieve."*

VIII

Fulfilling the Higher Objectives — The Path to Happiness in Both Worlds

Fulfilling the higher objectives of Sharia (maqāṣid) is the pathway to true happiness in both this world and the next, as it offers a holistic framework for human flourishing. These seven objectives—preserving religion, life, mind, lineage, wealth, homeland, and the unity of the Ummah—form the ethical and legal foundation of a just and balanced society. Each objective upholds essential aspects of human dignity and well-being: protecting faith as divine light, life as sacred trust, intellect as the basis of accountability, lineage as the bedrock of family, wealth as a means of honorable livelihood, homeland as the vessel of identity, and the Ummah as the bearer of divine purpose. When internalized and applied, these aims transform the individual into a conscious agent of peace and goodness. Through daily practice and strategic awareness, every believer can embody these principles—turning knowledge into action and society into a reflection of divine justice.

The Higher Objectives (Maqāṣid) of the Sharia

Introduction

Once the human being has been refined through the inward belief of *īmān*, the outward practice of *Islam*, and the spiritual excellence of *iḥsān*, the journey does not end. It expands—outward and upward. From personal purity emerges social justice. From individual servitude arises the framework for a just and compassionate civilization.

This transition is guided by the higher objectives (*maqāṣid*) of the Islamic Sharia: a divine blueprint not intended merely to regulate rituals, but to establish enduring principles that safeguard human dignity, nourish the soul, and build societies rooted in mercy.

Allah Almighty says:

> *"And We have not sent you, [O Muhammad], except as a mercy to the worlds."*
> (Qur'an, Al-Anbiyā' 21:107)

1. The Centrality of Maqāṣid in Islamic Legislation

The higher objectives of the Sharia are not abstract ideals—they are the very spirit behind Islamic law. Every divine command, from the most private ritual to the broadest political system, is designed to serve a greater purpose: the flourishing of human life under God's guidance.

As Imām al-Shāṭibī wrote in *Al-Muwāfaqāt*:

"The Sharia was established for the welfare of the people in this world and the next."

This welfare (*maṣlaḥah*) is not limited to material benefit—it encompasses moral, spiritual, intellectual, and social dimensions.

2. From the Individual to the Collective: A Civilizational Vision

The complete person formed through Islam, faith, and excellence is not meant to remain isolated. That transformation must ripple outward—into families, institutions, and nations.

Personal iḥsān becomes social justice.

Private devotion becomes public responsibility.

Only through the harmony of inner refinement and outward implementation can the objectives of Sharia be realized in full. This is how Islam moves from creed to culture, from personal salvation to societal elevation.

3. The Path to Happiness in Both Realms

Islamic law aims to establish two levels of happiness:

In this world — through:

- Justice and security
- Family stability
- Intellectual clarity
- Economic dignity
- Spiritual purpose

In the next — through:

- God's pleasure
- Deliverance from Hell
- Eternal life in Paradise

Allah says:

> *"Whoever does righteousness, whether male or female, while being a believer – We will surely grant them a good life."*
> (Qur'an, An-Naḥl 16:97)

4. The Core Objectives That Anchor the Sharia

In this section, we will explore the essential *maqāṣid*—those divine purposes upon which the entire framework of Islamic law rests:

1. **Preservation of Faith** – Anchoring the soul in divine truth and worship.
2. **Preservation of Life** – Protecting human dignity, safety, and well-being.
3. **Preservation of Intellect** – Ensuring access to truth and shielding against ignorance.
4. **Preservation of Lineage** – Building families and societies on moral

foundations.

5. **Preservation of Wealth** – Encouraging lawful prosperity and economic justice.
6. **Preservation of Homeland** – Safeguarding communal identity, security, and sovereignty.
7. **Preservation of the Ummah** – Reviving global unity, cooperation, and moral leadership among Muslims worldwide.

These are not merely legal categories—they are the heartbeat of a divinely guided civilization.

Conclusion:

The higher objectives of Sharia offer more than a legal system—they chart a roadmap from the individual soul to the universal society.

To uphold them is to turn worship into justice, spirituality into policy, and divine mercy into living reality.

To neglect them is to fragment religion into rituals without vision, or ethics without grounding.

The believer stands between two worlds. Let them walk with wisdom:

- Purifying the heart through *iḥsān,*
- And purifying society through justice and mercy.

For in fulfilling these divine objectives, we prepare not only for a better world—but for the eternal world to come.

> *"And whoever submits his face to Allah while being a doer of good – he has grasped the firmest handhold."*
> (Qur'an, Luqmān 31:22)

The Seven Higher Objectives of Sharia — A Framework for Human Flourishing

Introduction

Islamic law (*Sharia*) is not merely a set of isolated rulings; it is a comprehensive, divine blueprint for building just, ethical, and flourishing societies. Its goals are neither arbitrary nor outdated—they are timeless principles rooted in mercy, justice, and human dignity.

Scholars of *maqāṣid al-sharīʿah* (the higher objectives of Islamic law) have identified seven core aims that lie at the heart of this sacred legal system. These objectives serve to protect and promote what is essential for both the individual and society, in this life and the next.

Allah says:

> **"[This is] the color of Allah—and who is better than Allah in coloring?"**
> (*Qur'an, Al-Baqarah 2:138*)

1. What Are the Objectives of Sharia?

The *maqāṣid* are the higher purposes for which divine rulings were revealed. These objectives ensure the preservation of human well-being in all its dimensions—spiritual, moral, intellectual, and social.

As Imam al-Shāṭibī wrote:

"The purpose of Sharia is to guide the responsible human away from the pull of their lower desires, so that they may serve God by choice, just as they are His servant by nature."

2. Why Understanding the Maqasid Matters

- It deepens our understanding of Sharia beyond literal rulings.
- It allows for the wise and just application of divine law in different times and places.
- It helps scholars and communities balance between preserving timeless principles and responding to real-world challenges.

The *maqāṣid* ensure that law serves life, not the other way around.

3. The Seven Grand Objectives of Sharia

1. Preserving Faith and Worship (Dīn)

- Guarding belief in God and access to His guidance.
- Protecting the freedom to worship and live by divine values.

> *"I did not create jinn and mankind except to worship Me."*
> *(Qur'an, Adh-Dhāriyāt 51:56)*

2. Protecting Life and Human Dignity (Nafs)

- Upholding the sanctity of life.
- Establishing justice through laws that deter aggression and preserve security.

"Do not kill the soul which Allah has made sacred—except by right."
(Qur'an, Al-Isrā' 17:33)

3. Guarding Intellect and Reason ('Aql)

- Prohibiting substances and ideologies that corrupt the mind.
- Encouraging the pursuit of knowledge, reflection, and critical thought.

"Say: Are those who know equal to those who do not know?"
(Qur'an, Az-Zumar 39:9)

4. Honoring Family and Lineage (Nasl)

- Upholding the sanctity of marriage and family life.
- Prohibiting immorality and protecting the integrity of lineage.

"And of His signs is that He created for you from yourselves mates, that you may find tranquility in them."
(Qur'an, Ar-Rūm 30:21)

5. Securing Wealth and Economic Justice (Māl)

- Forbidding theft, fraud, and economic exploitation.
- Promoting lawful commerce, generosity, and financial integrity.

"Do not consume one another's wealth unjustly or send it [in bribery] to the rulers."
(Qur'an, Al-Baqarah 2:188)

6. Defending Land and Public Order (Watan)

- Safeguarding homeland, sacred sites, and national sovereignty.
- Encouraging defense of territory and the protection of civil peace.

"Prepare against them whatever forces you can..."
(Qur'an, Al-Anfāl 8:60)

7. Strengthening the Unity of the Ummah (Global Muslim Community)

- Promoting moral unity across cultures and nations.
- Resisting sectarianism and division.
- Supporting justice and compassion on a global scale.

"Hold firmly to the rope of Allah, all together, and do not be divided."
(Qur'an, Āl 'Imrān 3:103)

Conclusion: Toward a Civilization of Mercy

The seven objectives of Sharia are not just legal aims—they are civilizational pillars. They shape a world where:

- Divine guidance illuminates life,
- Justice prevails over oppression,
- And humanity flourishes in both spirit and structure.

When these objectives are realized, religion becomes more than worship—it becomes the architecture of mercy. It transforms faith into a lived reality and paves the way for lasting peace in this world, and eternal joy in the next.

Preservation of Religion — Safeguarding the Light of Divine Guidance

Introduction

At the forefront of the higher objectives (*maqāṣid*) of Islamic law stands the preservation of religion. This is not merely a legal concern, but the highest aim of the Sharia, and the first foundation upon which human well-being rests.

Religion connects the human being to their Creator and provides the spiritual, ethical, and existential compass for life. Without it, the purpose of existence becomes obscured, and divine responsibility collapses.

> **"So direct your face toward the religion, inclining to truth."**
> *(Qur'an, Ar-Rūm 30:30)*

1. What Does It Mean to Preserve Religion?

Preserving religion (*ḥifẓ al-dīn*) includes:

- Safeguarding correct beliefs from distortion, manipulation, or erasure.
- Protecting the freedom to practice rituals, ethics, and worship in safety.
- Ensuring access to authentic sources of revelation and knowledge.

- Preventing the marginalization or mockery of faith in public life.

To preserve religion is to preserve the divine light that guides humanity back to its Lord.

2. The Three Levels of Preservation

Islamic legal theory outlines three tiers of preservation:

a) Essential (Ḍarūrī) Level

This level safeguards the core pillars of faith and worship. It includes protection from ideological erasure, forced conversion, or mass persecution. In extreme cases, resistance is permitted to defend the ability to worship freely:

> **"Fight them until there is no [more] persecution and religion belongs wholly to Allah."**
> (Qur'an, Al-Anfāl 8:39)

This verse refers to defense, not conquest — ensuring no one is forced away from their faith.

b) Necessary (Ḥājī) Level

This involves facilitating religious learning, easing hardship in practice (e.g., concessions in illness or travel), and making faith accessible and livable for all.

c) Complementary (Taḥsīnī) Level

At this level, religion is not only protected but beautified — through virtuous character, compassionate da'wah, and living as a positive example. It aims to make faith attractive through wisdom and sincerity.

3. Practical Means of Preserving Religion

- **Education:** Teaching sound doctrine and critical understanding of religion from early childhood to adulthood.
- **Public Worship:** Protecting places of worship and enabling collective religious life.
- **Scholarship and Dialogue:** Defending religion from innovations, distortion, and extremism through reasoned and respectful discourse.
- **Calling to God:** Inviting others with wisdom, not force:

> **"Call to the way of your Lord with wisdom and good instruction."**
> *(Qur'an, An-Naḥl 16:125)*

4. Impact on Individuals and Society

Preserving religion leads to:

- **Spiritual clarity**: Individuals know their purpose and direction.
- **Moral grounding**: A society anchored in justice, mercy, and account-ability.
- **Cultural resilience**: Communities are protected from the erosion of their identity and values.
- **Worldly and eternal happiness**: Peace in this life and success in the Hereafter.

5. Contemporary Threats to Religious Preservation

Today, this objective faces new challenges:

- **Atheistic ideologies** that deny the soul or higher purpose.
- **Media narratives** that distort or vilify Islamic teachings.
- **Consumer culture** that distracts from faith and meaning.
- **Extremist interpretations** that misrepresent the religion from within.

In light of these, preserving religion requires not only scholarly defense but also living the faith with beauty, balance, and courage.

Conclusion

Preserving religion is not about enforcing rituals but about protecting humanity's access to divine truth. It is the light that gives meaning to existence, the path that leads to eternal joy, and the foundation of a just and compassionate society.

Whoever preserves this light walks with clarity and purpose.

Whoever neglects it risks losing both their soul and their way.

Preservation of Life — Human Dignity in the Scale of Islamic Law

Introduction

Following the preservation of religion, Islamic law upholds the sanctity of human life as one of its foremost objectives. Life is viewed not only as a biological phenomenon, but as a sacred trust from God — honored in creation, protected in law, and central to human responsibility.

Allah the Almighty says:

> *"And We have certainly honored the children of Adam."*
> **(Al-Isrā' 17:70)**

To preserve life is to safeguard the dignity, safety, and flourishing of every person — making it one of the cornerstones of justice and mercy in the divine legal framework.

1. What It Means to Preserve Life

Preserving life in Islamic law includes:

- Safeguarding people from murder, harm, or injustice.
- Providing essential needs: nourishment, health, and security.

- Establishing laws that prevent negligence, abuse, or violence.
- Upholding human dignity and prohibiting humiliation, exploitation, or oppression.

Life is not merely protected — it is honored. Its preservation is a shared duty across individuals, communities, and institutions.

2. Life's Elevated Status in the Sharia

Islamic law emphasizes the sanctity of life through:

- Prohibitions on unlawful killing.
- Retributive justice (qisās) to deter and remedy violent crimes.
- Compensation laws (diyah) to uphold accountability.
- Forbidding self-harm, suicide, and reckless endangerment.
- Protecting related dignities, such as intellect and honor.

Allah says:

> *"And do not kill yourselves. Surely Allah is Most Merciful to you."*
> **(An-Nisā' 4:29)**

These protections aim not only to preserve existence, but to cultivate a just and life-affirming society.

3. Means of Preserving Life in Practice

Islam provides multifaceted safeguards for life, including:

Prohibition of Unjust Killing

"Whoever kills a person unjustly... it is as if he has killed all mankind."
(Al-Māʾidah 5:32)

Qisās (Retributive Justice)

"And in retribution there is [saving of] life for you."
(Al-Baqarah 2:179)

Social Solidarity and Care

Ensuring access to food, shelter, security, and healthcare — a communal and state responsibility.

Prohibition of Suicide and Self-Harm

Preserving life includes caring for mental health, preventing despair, and forbidding self-destruction.

Emphasis on Treatment and Healing

Accessing medicine and seeking healing is encouraged — even obligatory — when life is at stake.

These measures reflect Islam's holistic view: preserving life encompasses both protecting it from harm and nurturing it toward well-being.

4. Societal Impact of Life Preservation

When life is upheld as sacred:

- Societies become secure, stable, and just.
- Mutual respect grows among individuals and communities.
- Space is created for creativity, growth, and dignity.
- The weak and vulnerable are protected, and violence is minimized.

The Prophet ﷺ said:

> "The destruction of the world is less serious in the sight of Allah
> than the unjust killing of a believer."
> **(Reported by al-Nasā'ī)**

The spirit of Sharia is not mere punishment but the prevention of injustice
before it begins.

5. Contemporary Threats to Life

Today, the preservation of life faces complex challenges:

- Unjust wars and civilian casualties
- Acts of terrorism and suicide attacks
- Organized violence and systemic neglect
- Environmental hazards and public health crises

These issues call for renewed application of maqāṣid-based thinking —
grounding legal responses in the spirit of life-preserving justice, not just
technical rulings.

Conclusion

Preserving life in Islam is not just a legal principle — it is a divine imperative and moral commitment. It affirms the God-given worth of every soul and enshrines mercy, dignity, and safety as foundations of any righteous society.

Whoever protects life fulfills one of the highest trusts of creation. And whoever nurtures it brings light to the world — walking the path of God's mercy and the prophetic legacy of compassion.

Preservation of the Mind — Safeguarding the Center of Thought and Choice

Introduction

Among the highest aims of Islamic law is the preservation of the human intellect — not merely as a biological function, but as the divine faculty by which we recognize truth, choose meaning, and ascend toward our Creator. The intellect is the lamp of human awareness, the foundation of moral accountability, and the gateway to both religious understanding and civilizational advancement.

Without the mind, there is no recognition of God, no discernment between truth and falsehood, and no fulfillment of divine responsibility. Hence, Islamic law (Sharī'ah) honors the mind by protecting, nurturing, and guiding it.

Allah the Almighty says:

"Will you not then use your reason?" (Qur'an, *Al-Baqarah* 2:44)

"Will you not then reflect?" (Qur'an, *Al-An'ām* 6:50)

1. What It Means to Preserve the Mind

To preserve the intellect is to:

- Safeguard it from physical, psychological, or ideological harm.
- Protect thought from stagnation, manipulation, or extremism.
- Nurture it with sound knowledge, deep reflection, and spiritual clarity.
- Encourage inquiry while grounding it in humility before divine truth.

The mind is not just a tool of cognition—it is a spiritual trust. Through it, the human being knows their Lord and becomes a builder of justice and wisdom on earth.

2. The Status of the Intellect in Revelation

The Qur'an speaks repeatedly to the mind — calling it to observe, reflect, question, and reason.

> **"And they reflect upon the creation of the heavens and the earth..."** (Qur'an, Āl 'Imrān 3:191)

The Prophet ﷺ also honored deep thinking, saying:

> *"Reflect upon the blessings of Allah, but do not reflect upon His Essence." (Reported by al-Ṭabarānī)*

This emphasis elevates reflection and reasoning to acts of devotion, binding intellect and spirituality together.

3. Means of Preserving the Mind in Islamic Law

Encouraging the Pursuit of Knowledge

- Knowledge is the nourishment of the intellect and the foundation of ethical civilization.

"Say: Are those who know equal to those who do not know?"
(Qur'an, *Az-Zumar* 39:9)

Prohibiting Intoxicants and Substances That Impair Thought

- Islam forbids wine and drugs because they cloud reason and disrupt moral judgment.

"Every intoxicant is prohibited." (*Reported by Muslim*)

Promoting Sound Thought and Discouraging Distortion

- Sharī'ah encourages clarity, warns against confusion, and defends the mind from extremism and misguidance.

Supporting Critical Thinking and Constructive Innovation

- Islam invites *ijtihād* (independent reasoning) within divine bounds, empowering minds to address new challenges with wisdom and insight.

4. Impact on Individuals and Society

When the mind is preserved and cultivated:

- Faith becomes deep-rooted, not superficial.
- Individuals make wise, ethical decisions.

- Communities thrive on knowledge, creativity, and justice.
- Societies can resist ignorance, injustice, and ideological manipulation.

The Prophet ﷺ said:

> *"When Allah intends good for someone, He grants them under-standing of the religion."* (Agreed upon)

5. Contemporary Challenges to Mental Integrity

Today, the preservation of the mind faces unprecedented threats:

- **Ideological manipulation** through misinformation and digital over-load
- **Normalization of self-harm** and escapism through drugs or hyper-stimulation
- **Suppression of critical thought** in favor of blind imitation or secular extremism
- **Intellectual colonization**, undermining moral frameworks in the name of progress

These issues demand renewed educational, spiritual, and legal efforts to protect and restore the integrity of human thought.

Conclusion

To preserve the intellect is to honor the very gift that sets humanity apart — the power to know truth, choose rightly, and seek God with clarity. It is through the mind that revelation is understood, ethics are applied, and civilization is advanced.

Whoever cultivates their intellect through faith, knowledge, and sincere reflection walks a path of light. But whoever abandons or corrupts their mind risks wandering in confusion and loss.

Let us then preserve this noble trust — not just for ourselves, but for the generations that follow — so that guidance, wisdom, and truth may continue to illuminate the world.

Preservation of Lineage — Building a Pure Family and Society

Introduction

Among the noblest objectives of Islamic law—after the preservation of religion, life, and intellect—is the preservation of lineage.

Lineage is not merely a biological record; it is the sacred thread through which human identity, moral legacy, and divine trust are passed from one generation to the next.

It is the foundation of *khilāfah* (succession) on earth, the framework for family and community life, and a guarantee of continuity grounded in purity, justice, and dignity.

Allah the Almighty says:

> "O mankind! Be mindful of your Lord, who created you from a single soul, and from it created its mate, and from the two spread many men and women..."
>
> **(An-Nisāʾ 4:1)**

1. The Meaning of Preserving Lineage

Preserving lineage means safeguarding the integrity of family and the moral order that supports it. This includes:

1. Establishing lawful family structures through valid and ethical marriage.
2. Guaranteeing children the right to their true parentage, care, and a stable upbringing.
3. Prohibiting actions that blur or distort lineage through immorality or exploitation.
4. Implementing legal protections that support family stability and uphold generational trust.

To preserve lineage is to protect the very soil in which moral values, religious identity, and social harmony are cultivated.

2. The Status of Lineage in Islamic Law

Lineage is not simply about reproduction—it is a spiritual and civilizational mission.

Through lineage, faith is passed on, cultures are preserved, and generations are shaped by shared memory and moral responsibility.

The Prophet ﷺ said:

> *"Marry affectionate and fertile women, for I will boast of your numbers before the nations on the Day of Resurrection."*
> **(Reported by Abū Dāwūd)**

Righteous offspring are among the manifestations of divine mercy on earth, and raising them in faith is among the greatest acts of worship.

3. Means of Preserving Lineage in Islam

Islamic law provides clear mechanisms to safeguard lineage, including:

Marriage as a Sacred Covenant

- A divine bond that legitimizes family formation and ensures moral grounding.

  "Marry off those among you who are single..." (*An-Nūr 24:32*)

Guarding Moral Boundaries

- Islam forbids all acts that compromise the clarity and dignity of family structure, such as fornication and same-sex sexual relations, while encouraging repentance and reform.

  "Do not go near fornication. It is truly a shameful deed and an evil way." (*Al-Isrā' 17:32*)

Upholding Laws of Parentage, Inheritance, and Custody

- These protect the legal, emotional, and financial rights of children.

Honoring the Rights of Children

- Every child is entitled to nurturing care, moral education, and a life of dignity in alignment with their innate *fiṭrah*.

4. The Impact of Preserving Lineage on Society

When lineage is protected and family life is honored, society reaps profound benefits:

- The formation of loving, stable families rooted in mercy and mutual respect.
- Protection against social disintegration, alienation, and moral confusion.
- Preservation of religious identity and transmission of values across generations.
- Strengthening the foundations of social justice, compassion, and community cohesion.

5. Contemporary Challenges to Lineage Preservation

In today's world, the preservation of lineage faces unprecedented threats:

- The normalization of extramarital relationships and rejection of traditional marriage.
- The rise of legally questionable or exploitative marriage arrangements.
- Increasing neglect of children's religious and ethical education.
- Cultural shifts that attempt to redefine or dissolve the concept of family itself.

These challenges demand not only legal clarity but a spiritual and educational response that revives the sanctity of family life and the centrality of lineage in human flourishing.

Conclusion

Preserving lineage is more than protecting names and records—it is about honoring the human soul, sustaining the moral fabric of society, and securing a righteous future.

It ensures that each generation is born into clarity, raised in mercy, and rooted in values that serve both God and humanity.

Whoever preserves lineage through lawful marriage, moral integrity, and conscious parenting fulfills a divine trust and contributes to the creation of a just and compassionate civilization.

In a world increasingly unmoored from traditional anchors, the Islamic vision of family offers a sanctuary of clarity, mercy, and sacred purpose.

Preservation of Wealth — A Guarantee of Economic and Social Dignity

Introduction

In the holistic framework of Islamic law, the preservation of wealth stands as one of its highest objectives. Wealth is not an end in itself, but a means of sustaining dignified life, enabling social cohesion, and fostering justice. It is a divine trust (*amānah*)—meant to be protected, ethically developed, and used in ways that benefit both the individual and society.

Allah the Almighty says:

> **"Do not entrust the incapable with your wealth, which Allah has made a means of support for you..."**
> (*An-Nisā' 4:5*)

By safeguarding wealth, Islamic law ensures not only financial security but also human dignity and social harmony.

1. The Meaning of Preserving Wealth

Preserving wealth means:

1. Protecting it from theft, fraud, corruption, or unlawful seizure.

2. Earning it through lawful (*ḥalāl*) and ethical means.
3. Managing and spending it in ways that align with the moral and legal guidelines of Islam.
4. Prohibiting exploitative practices such as usury (*riba*), deceit, and economic manipulation.

Wealth, in this sense, is the backbone of civilization and a resource for service—not a personal idol. The way it is acquired and spent determines its spiritual value.

2. The Importance of Wealth in the Islamic Perspective

Islam recognizes wealth as a tool—not inherently good or evil—but morally neutral and judged by its purpose and usage. It can uplift or degrade depending on intention and action.

The Prophet ﷺ said:

> *"Blessed is the righteous wealth for a righteous person."*
> (Narrated by Aḥmad)

Wealth enables charitable giving, supports communal development, and fulfills familial and societal obligations. When managed with sincerity and integrity, it becomes a powerful means to serve both God and creation.

3. Means of Preserving Wealth in Islamic Law

Islamic teachings offer a robust system for wealth preservation, including:

• **Prohibiting unjust gain**: Theft, bribery, embezzlement, fraud, and other forms of economic exploitation are categorically forbidden.

"Do not consume one another's wealth unjustly..." (Al-Baqarah 2:188)

- **Enacting deterrent laws**: The *ḥadd* for theft and legal recourse for financial abuse aim to protect both public and private property.
- **Regulating transactions**: Islamic law encourages lawful contracts (sales, leasing, partnerships, endowments, wills) that are transparent, consensual, and just.
- **Mandating zakat and encouraging ṣadaqah**:
- Zakat—unlike voluntary charity—is an obligatory redistribution tool that purifies wealth and alleviates poverty, making wealth a collective responsibility.
- **Encouraging productive investment**: Islam promotes trade, agriculture, and industry, provided they are free from exploitation and serve the broader good.

4. The Impact of Preserving Wealth on Individuals and Society

- **Secures individual dignity** by ensuring people have access to their needs without humiliation.
- **Creates a stable, just society**, where economic rights are respected and protected.
- **Strengthens social solidarity**, as those with excess give to those in need.
- **Builds thriving communities** where ethical productivity and lawful exchange are the norm.

In this way, wealth becomes a vehicle of upliftment—not oppression.

5. Contemporary Threats to Wealth Preservation

Despite these protections, wealth today is under new pressures that require revival and renewal of Islamic economic principles:

- Financial corruption and administrative embezzlement
- Exploitation through *riba*, monopolies, and predatory speculation
- Mismanagement of public funds
- Rampant consumerism and the erosion of ethical restraint

These threats highlight the need for faith-based economic education, institutional reform, and the development of *maqāṣid*-based financial systems that uphold justice and balance.

Conclusion

The preservation of wealth is a foundational objective in Islamic law that safeguards individual rights and social wellbeing. It ensures that wealth circulates justly, fulfills responsibilities, and uplifts communities rather than deepening inequality.

Whoever manages wealth as a trust from Allah—earning it lawfully, spending it ethically, and sharing it generously—walks the path of *istikhlāf* (divine stewardship) and contributes to a just, spiritually grounded civilization.

Preserving the Homeland — Safeguarding Land and Identity

Introduction

Within the higher objectives (*maqāṣid*) of Islamic law, the preservation of the homeland holds an exalted place. The homeland is far more than a geographical location—it is the vessel in which faith, dignity, and identity are safeguarded, and where the divine purposes of the Sharīʿah are realized in practice.

Defending one's homeland is not merely an act of patriotism; it is a sacred duty. It is through this protection that the broader aims of Islamic law—faith, life, intellect, lineage, and wealth—are maintained and civilizations allowed to flourish.

Allah says, through the words of Moses (peace be upon him):

> *"He said, 'My Lord, save me from the wrongdoing people.'"*
> *(Al-Qaṣaṣ 28:21)*

1. The Meaning of Preserving the Homeland

Preserving the homeland entails:

- Defending it from occupation and aggression.
- Safeguarding its religious, cultural, and moral identity.
- Strengthening national unity and preventing internal division.
- Ensuring political and economic security and independence.

The homeland is the shield of identity and the ground upon which divine values are nurtured and upheld.

2. The Status of the Homeland in Islam

Islamic sources emphasize the virtue of loving and defending one's land. When the Prophet ﷺ was forced to leave Makkah, he expressed profound love for it, saying:

> "By Allah, you are the most beloved land of Allah to me, and had your people not expelled me, I would never have left you."
> (Narrated by al-Tirmidhī)

Defending the homeland—particularly when it is under threat—is not only a legal right but a religious obligation.

> *"Fight in the way of Allah those who fight you..."*
> *(Al-Baqarah 2:190)*

3. Means of Preserving the Homeland in Islamic Law

Lawful Patriotism

- Loving and serving one's homeland in a way that honors Islamic principles and avoids tribalism or injustice.

Legitimate Defense

- Repelling aggression and occupation is among the noblest forms of worship.

The Prophet ﷺ said:

> "Whoever is killed defending his wealth is a martyr; whoever is killed defending his family is a martyr; whoever is killed defending his life is a martyr."
> (Narrated by al-Tirmidhī)

Nation-Building

- Through knowledge, ethics, economic strength, and just governance.

Combating Internal Corruption and Disorder

- Maintaining the rule of law, promoting unity, and protecting against sabotage and civil strife.

4. Homeland Preservation as a Pillar of Other Objectives

Preserving the homeland ensures the success of other *maqāṣid*:

- **Religion**: A protected land enables free worship and the application of Islamic values.
- **Life**: Stability protects against chaos and bloodshed.
- **Intellect**: A safe environment fosters education and critical thinking.
- **Lineage**: Strong families are built in secure, supportive communities.
- **Wealth**: Economic growth and protection of property require peace and order.
- **Ummah**: Sovereignty preserves the dignity and collective identity of Muslims.

"And hold firmly to the rope of Allah all together and do not become divided."
(Āl ʿImrān 3:103)

5. Contemporary Threats to the Homeland

- Foreign occupation and aggression
- Civil wars and sectarian conflict
- Cultural and ideological subversion
- Political and economic corruption
- Environmental degradation and neglect

These threats demand vigilant awareness, unified action, and a return to values rooted in divine guidance and national integrity.

Conclusion:

Preserving the homeland is among the greatest religious and moral responsibilities. It is not simply an act of national defense, but an act of *'ibādah*—a sacred trust that ensures the protection of all other divine objectives.

To safeguard one's homeland is to safeguard religion, identity, and the future of generations. Whoever rises to this responsibility does not merely serve their nation—they fulfill a divine duty and walk the path of honor, sacrifice, and divine reward.

Preserving the Ummah — Unity of Ranks and Continuity of the Divine Message

Introduction

At the summit of the higher objectives (*maqāṣid*) of Islamic law stands the preservation of the *Ummah*—not merely as a collection of individuals, but as a living, God-appointed community entrusted with upholding justice and conveying mercy to the world.

This collective is the final bearer of divine guidance, the witness over all nations, and the standard-bearer of moral truth on Earth. Preserving the Ummah means safeguarding its existence, unity, and spiritual mission—ensuring that its light continues to guide humanity.

Allah says:

> *"Thus We have made you a just and balanced nation, so that you may be witnesses over humanity."*
> (Al-Baqarah 2:143)

1. The Meaning of Preserving the Ummah

Preserving the Ummah includes:

- Guarding its religious, political, and cultural unity from fragmentation.
- Upholding its core message—faith, ethics, and justice—against distortion.
- Resisting internal discord and sectarianism that tear at its fabric.
- Reinforcing its strength through knowledge, stability, and independence.
- Elevating its global role as a source of light, equity, and compassion.

The *Ummah* is not just a community; it is a sacred trust, a witness to God's truth on Earth.

2. The Scriptural Emphasis on Unity

Islamic texts deeply emphasize preserving the Ummah's cohesion:

> *"Do not be like those who became divided and differed after clear proofs had come to them."*
> (Āl 'Imrān 3:105)

When the Prophet ﷺ said,

> "The Hand of Allah is with the community,"
> *(Reported by al-Tirmidhī)*

he was reminding us that divine support is tied to collective unity.

Division is not a mere disagreement—it is a spiritual and existential threat to the mission of Islam.

3. Means of Preserving the Ummah

Preservation requires a multi-layered approach rooted in Sharia:

Unity of Belief and Methodology:

- Grounding our thought and practice in the Qur'an and Sunnah while rejecting extremes and ideological deviation.

Brotherhood and Social Solidarity:

- Living the verse:

"Indeed, the believers are but brothers." (Al-Ḥujurāt 49:10)

through mercy, justice, and compassion.

Preventing and Resolving Conflict:

- Striving for peaceful reform, dialogue, and reconciliation, especially in times of tension.

Building Civilizational Capacity:

- Advancing knowledge, economic strength, and political stability in service of Islam's values.

Upholding Shūrā and Justice:

- Governance based on consultation, fairness, and transparency is essential to prevent tyranny and foster trust.

4. Why Preserving the Ummah Matters to the World

A united and principled *Ummah* is a beacon for all of humanity—showing that a civilization rooted in revelation can offer mercy, wisdom, and ethical leadership.

But when the Ummah falters—fractured by conflict or diluted by alien ideologies—it opens the door for tyranny, injustice, and spiritual darkness to prevail.

The Prophet ﷺ said:

> "The example of my Ummah is like that of rain—one does not know whether the first part or the last part is better."
> *(Narrated by al-Tirmidhī)*

This reminds us that renewal is always possible, and hope is never lost.

5. Contemporary Threats to the Ummah

Today, the Ummah faces profound and complex challenges:

- **Sectarianism and ethnic conflict** weaken its spiritual core.
- **Ideological colonization** distorts its identity.
- **Cultural fragmentation** erodes its values through unchecked globalization.
- **Injustice and political corruption** disillusion its people and fracture its unity.

These threats demand a holistic revival—a renewal rooted in the timeless guidance of the Qur'an and Sunnah, carried by hearts sincere in love for their faith and community.

Conclusion:

To preserve the Ummah is to preserve the final divine message given to humanity.

It is to shield the last light of guidance from extinction and to ensure that justice and mercy remain possible in a broken world.

Whoever contributes to the unity, resilience, and flourishing of the Ummah safeguards not only religion but the future of humanity itself.

Let us rise as builders of that sacred bond, and as stewards of the divine trust that began with the Prophet ﷺ and continues through us—until the Final Hour.

How a Person Can Fulfill the Higher Objectives of Sharia in Daily Life

Introduction

Every believer longs for a life of meaning—one that connects the soul to its Creator while serving the world with integrity.

The higher objectives (*maqāṣid*) of Islamic law are not abstract ideals or distant philosophical constructs;

they are divine signposts meant to guide us through daily life with clarity, purpose, and grace.

These objectives offer more than rules; they offer a vision—of a life aligned with sacred purpose,

a civilization rooted in mercy and justice,

and a journey that transforms the ordinary into acts of nearness to God. Allah says:

> *"Say, indeed my prayer, my worship, my life, and my death are for Allah, Lord of the worlds."*
> *(Al-Anʿām 6:162)*

1. Transforming Objectives into Conscious Living

When a believer understands the *maqāṣid*, they gain not only knowledge but perspective:

- Every action becomes a means of preserving divine purpose.
- Every moment becomes a chance to serve the higher good.
- Every decision is weighed by both its effect in this world and its weight in the next.

To live by the *maqāṣid* is to move from blind ritualism to conscious faith, where ethics, worship, and social responsibility become unified.

2. Applying the Objectives of Sharia in Everyday Life

Preserving Religion

- Pray with sincerity, not habit.
- Seek and share sacred knowledge.
- Reflect faith in manners, speech, and compassion.

Preserving Life

- Care for your health—body and mind.
- Respect others' lives and safety.
- Work to build safe, just communities.

Preserving Intellect

- Pursue beneficial knowledge.
- Reject mind-altering substances.
- Foster a culture of reflection rooted in revelation.

Preserving Lineage

- Uphold the dignity of marriage.
- Raise children with moral clarity.
- Protect the family from corrosive cultural forces.

Preserving Wealth

- Earn honestly.
- Spend mindfully.
- Give generously.

Preserving the Homeland

- Defend your society with action, ideas, and service.
- Uplift your nation with knowledge and integrity.
- Avoid civil discord and promote reform through wisdom.

Preserving the Ummah

- Strive for unity with mercy, not uniformity through force.
- Support just causes with your voice, hands, or resources.
- Practice brotherhood that transcends race, class, and sect.

3. Iḥsān — The Spirit of Every Objective

Iḥsān is the soul of Sharia's objectives.

- It turns duty into devotion.
- It transforms work into worship.
- It beautifies action with sincerity and depth.

The Prophet ﷺ said:

"Allah has prescribed excellence (iḥsān) in everything."
(Narrated by Muslim)

Living with iḥsān means striving for God's pleasure in every intention,
and in every interaction—seen or unseen.

4. Facing the Modern Challenges

Today's world makes mindful practice difficult:

- Materialism drowns the soul in distraction.
- Social media numbs spiritual awareness.
- Many feel pulled between tradition and modern pressures.
- Role models are rare, and moral clarity is often blurred.

But the believer's strength lies in spiritual resilience:
reconnecting with purpose, surrounding themselves with truth,
and returning—again and again—to Allah's light.

Conclusion: A Life of Purpose, A Journey to God

To live by the higher objectives of Sharia is to live awake.
It is to walk this earth as a servant, a reformer, and a lover of truth.
It is to turn every step—whether in worship, work, or family—into a step
toward eternity.
"Every moment lived with purpose is a moment that echoes in the Hereafter."
Let your life be a mirror of divine mercy.
Let your actions bear the fragrance of God's guidance.
And let every breath carry you closer to the One who created you in love
and awaits you in mercy.

Practical Strategies for Implementing the Higher Objectives of Sharia

Introduction

The higher objectives (*maqāṣid*) of Islamic law are not distant ideals confined to academic discourse or religious theory. They are meant to guide every dimension of life—illuminating our daily actions, shaping our communities, and refining our character.

To bring these divine aims into lived reality, we must move beyond passive belief into intentional, structured implementation. With purpose, planning, and excellence, these objectives can elevate both individual lives and entire societies.

Allah says:

> **"Say, 'Act, for Allah will see your deeds...'"**
> (*At-Tawbah* 9:105)

1. Intentional Awareness: Begin Every Action with Purpose

A believer's mindset is not limited to outward behavior—it begins with inward clarity. Every action should be framed by a conscious intent to serve one of the higher objectives:

- Eating or exercising becomes an act of **preserving life**.
- Studying and reflection become paths to **preserving intellect**.
- Earning honestly and giving generously fulfill the aim of **preserving wealth**.

This awareness transforms routine acts into acts of worship and service to the divine order.

2. Setting Daily Goals Inspired by the Maqāṣid

Build a life guided by clear, intentional habits. Align your everyday practices with the objectives of Sharia:

- **Prayer and fasting** → Preserving faith
- **Health and rest** → Preserving life
- **Reading and reflection** → Preserving intellect
- **Time with family** → Preserving lineage
- **Smart spending and saving** → Preserving wealth
- **Volunteering or civic work** → Preserving the homeland
- **Advocating for truth and unity** → Preserving the Ummah

Even small, regular actions can be powerful when rooted in divine purpose.

3. Cultivating Collective Awareness Across Society

To revive the maqāṣid, we must go beyond the personal and nurture a shared moral consciousness:

- In **homes**, teach children the purpose behind faith.
- In **schools and universities**, connect subjects to higher ethical aims.
- In **media**, promote truth, dignity, and constructive narratives.
- In **mosques**, deliver sermons that merge spiritual insight with actionable guidance.

As the Prophet ﷺ said:

"The religion is sincere advice." (Narrated by Muslim)

4. Embedding the Objectives in Our Social and Professional Roles

Every role in society can reflect the maqāṣid when guided by integrity:

- A **public official** ensures justice and protects communal resources.
- A **judge** upholds fairness, defending life and dignity.
- A **teacher or scholar** nurtures intellect and inspires critical thought.
- A **business owner** honors contracts, spreads wealth ethically, and contributes to social stability.

No profession is too mundane—every effort counts when directed toward divine ends.

5. Progress with Patience, Excellence, and Vision

Spiritual and social transformation requires **gradual effort and sustained excellence (iḥsān)**:

- Begin with yourself—then uplift your family, workplace, and community.
- Don't rush. Excellence is not achieved overnight, but through sincerity and steadiness.
- Let every step be marked by quality, not just quantity.

Allah says:

> **"And worship your Lord until certainty [death] comes to you."**
> (*Al-Ḥijr* 15:99)

Conclusion:

To implement the higher objectives of Sharia is to live with vision, depth, and divine alignment. It is to turn worship into purpose, and purpose into progress.

With sincere intent, strategic action, and steadfast commitment, every believer can become a torchbearer of mercy, justice, and revival. They do not merely follow the law—they embody its light.

Whoever walks this path becomes a builder of conscience, a guardian of their Ummah, and a seeker of Allah's eternal pleasure.

The Human Being as a Maker of Inner and Outer Peace

Introduction

In the comprehensive vision of Islam, the human being is not simply a seeker of peace—but a creator of it. Islam calls the believer to radiate peace:

- Within the heart,
- With the Creator,
- Among people,
- And across the natural world.

At its essence, Islam is a divine invitation to wholeness and harmony. **Allah says:**

> *"And Allah invites to the Home of Peace..."*
> (Qur'an, Yunus 10:25)

1. Inner Peace — The Foundation of Growth

Peace begins within. A soul at rest can heal others; a conflicted soul cannot. Achieving peace with oneself requires:

1. **Cleansing the heart** of confusion and despair through certainty in God.
2. **Embracing divine decree** with trust, letting go of resentment and inner conflict.
3. **Nurturing noble qualities** like patience, gratitude, contentment, and humility.

Allah says:

> *"Truly, it is in the remembrance of Allah that hearts find rest."*
> (Qur'an, Ar-Ra'd 13:28)

A tranquil inner world becomes the seedbed for justice, compassion, and clarity in the outer world.

2. Peace with God — The Heart of Faith

Peace with Allah is not merely emotional—it is existential. It is the soul's rest in its true home.

This peace comes through:

- **Tawḥīd (pure monotheism),** affirming Allah's oneness,
- **Surrendering the ego** in loving submission to His will,
- **Walking faithfully** in His light even when the road is difficult.

Allah says:

> *"Yes, whoever submits his face to Allah while doing good... his reward is with his Lord."*
> (Qur'an, Al-Baqarah 2:112)

The more rooted one's faith, the deeper the stillness of the soul.

3. Peace with People — The Muslim's Mission

A true Muslim radiates safety. Others feel shielded from harm—by word or deed—when near them.

This peace is built through:

- Thoughtful speech,
- Just actions,
- Kindness even in disagreement,
- Courage in resisting injustice—lawfully and ethically.

The Prophet 攤 said:

> "The Muslim is the one from whose tongue and hand people are safe."
> *(Reported by Bukhārī and Muslim)*

The Prophet 攤's life offers vivid examples—from forgiving his persecutors in Makkah to comforting the oppressed. Peace is not weakness. It is mercy infused with justice.

4. Peace with the Universe — Living as a Steward

The believer sees the world not as a possession but a trust (amānah). Peace with the earth is part of worship.

Islam calls for:

- **Sustainable living,**
- **Respect for animals,**
- **Avoiding corruption and excess,**
- **Protecting the balance of ecosystems.**

Allah says:

> *"And do not cause corruption on the earth after it has been set in order."*
> (Qur'an, Al-A'rāf 7:56)

From planting a tree to conserving water, every mindful act is part of a sacred ecology.

5. Practical Strategies for Building Peace

- Begin your day with **dhikr** to center the soul.
- Practice **gentleness and forgiveness** even when hurt.
- Step forward to **reconcile conflict** with wisdom.
- Choose **dialogue over dispute.**
- Support **justice and compassion** in your community.

Conclusion:

A sincere Muslim is:

- A cultivator of **inner peace**, shaped by faith and surrender,
- A peacemaker in **society**, through mercy and justice,
- A steward of **creation**, guided by reverence and responsibility.

Whoever sows peace with their hands, heart, and words—
will harvest God's peace in the Hereafter.
They will be welcomed not just into a tranquil world,
but into the *Dar al-Salām*—**the eternal Home of Peace.**

IX

The Final Conclusion

The final conclusion of this work is a comprehensive call to understand and actively engage in the full journey of the human being—from origin to destiny—with faith, purpose, and awareness. It is an invitation to rise above passive existence and live a life grounded in deep spiritual insight, moral excellence, and sincere action. By recognizing one's role as a conscious servant of God and a responsible member of humanity, each person is urged to walk the path of faith, cultivate inner growth, and contribute meaningfully to the world—transforming knowledge into lived purpose and awakening into a life of higher meaning.

From Divine Trust to Eternal Destiny

Introduction

This book has been a reflection on the complete human journey—
    from the divine origin to the eternal destination.
    We began with the knowledge of God the Creator,
    traced the mystery of existence,
    and walked through the stages of the human being's path:
    birth, life, death, resurrection, and judgment.
    Then we rose to the highest goals—
    living the fullness of **Islam**, deepening **faith**, striving for **iḥsān**,
    and embodying the **higher objectives (maqāṣid)** of the divine law.
    From this, we glimpsed the image of the complete human—
    a servant of God,
    a builder of peace,
    a traveler toward eternity.

1. The Human Being: Between Trust and Responsibility

Human life is not accidental.
  We were created with purpose,
  entrusted with the greatest trust of all:
  the trust of guidance, will, and moral responsibility.

"Indeed, We offered the Trust to the heavens and the earth and the mountains,
  and they declined to bear it and feared it; but man undertook it."
  (*Qur'an, Al-Aḥzāb 33:72*)

Each soul carries the weight of:

- **Faith,**
- **Righteous action,**
- **And bearing witness to truth.**

To be human is to be accountable—
  to live awake.

2. The Purpose of Existence: To Know and Worship God

The journey finds its meaning in a single truth:

> "I did not create jinn and humans except to worship Me."
> (*Qur'an, Adh-Dhāriyāt 51:56*)

But this worship is not ritual alone.
  It is a way of seeing, living, and walking—
  A life of prayer, justice, sincerity, and love
  that flows through the heart into every deed.
  To worship is to *know* God,
  to *love* Him,
  and to orient the soul toward its eternal Beloved.

3. Fulfilling the Mission in Everyday Life

A faithful servant lives the purpose of the journey by:

- Preserving **faith** through tawḥīd (oneness) and sincerity.
- Preserving **life** through care, modesty, and protection.
- Preserving **intellect** through learning and reflection.
- Preserving **family** through purity and love.
- Preserving **wealth** through honesty and gratitude.
- Preserving the **homeland** through justice and responsibility.
- Preserving the **ummah** through unity and compassion.

These actions are not abstract ideals.
  They are how a person walks the path to God
  —in this world, and beyond it.

4. The Final Destiny: The Abode of Permanence

After life ends, the soul arrives at the edge of eternity.

> "Whoever is removed from the Fire and admitted to Paradise—he has succeeded."
> *(Qur'an, Āl ʿImrān 3:185)*

- For the believer, there is **nearness to God,**
- joy beyond imagination,
- and peace that never fades.
- For the heedless, there is **regret,**
- distance from mercy,
- and a fire that never dies.

The decisions made in this short life echo forever.
Eternity is shaped by the sincerity of the present moment.

5. A Final Invitation to You, Dear Reader

You have now traveled through the story of your own existence.
You know who you are.
You know why you were created.
You know where you are going.
And in your hands lies the map—
its signposts are:
God. Faith. Action. Mercy. Peace.
So begin.
Step forward with a sound heart,
with deeds of beauty,
with eyes fixed on eternity.

"O tranquil soul, return to your Lord—pleased and pleasing.
Enter among My servants.
Enter My Paradise."
(Qur'an, Al-Fajr 89:27–30)

Final Summary: The Journey of Light

The journey of the human being
    is a journey of **trust**
    a journey of **choice**,
    a journey of **return**.
    It begins in divine breath.
    It passes through a world of trials and gifts.
    And it ends at the gate of forever.
    So let your life become a bridge to eternity.
    Let your hands carry the light of mercy.
    Let your voice bear witness to truth.
    Let your heart remain always awake to your Lord.
    On the Day when neither wealth nor children will avail,
    only those who come to God with a sound heart will succeed.
    Let that heart be yours.

A Comprehensive Call to Understand the Full Journey of the Human Being

Introduction

In a world shaken by uncertainty and overwhelmed by distraction, many search for a compass—something to anchor the soul and clarify the path.

From this deep need arises a comprehensive invitation:

a call to embark on a full intellectual and spiritual journey—

one that begins before time itself and stretches beyond it,

charting the complete human path through the lens of both revelation and reason.

> *"Did you think that We created you in vain and that to Us you would not be returned?"*
> **(Al-Mu'minūn 23:115)**

1. Why Understanding the Full Path Is an Existential Necessity

When a person is unaware of their origin, their purpose, and their ultimate destination, they drift—lost in confusion, driven by passing desires, and overwhelmed by temporary concerns.

But when they understand:

- **Where they came from,**
- **Why they were created,**
- **Where they are going,**

their life becomes upright, their humanity elevated, and their heart prepared to meet its Creator with clarity and hope.

2. The Components of the Human Journey

- **God** — the Absolute Truth and the ultimate destination.
- **Creation** — the unfolding of divine will and wisdom.
- **The Universe** — a living sign open to reflection.
- **The Human Being** — a bearer of trust, endowed with freedom and responsibility.
- **Birth and Life** — the station of trial and purpose.
- **Death and the Grave** — the passage into the unseen.
- **Resurrection and Judgment** — the unveiling of all truth.
- **Paradise or Hell** — the final and eternal abode.

Each phase flows into the next in a seamless, divinely ordained sequence—linking the temporary with the eternal.

3. How to Understand the Complete Human Journey

To truly grasp this path, a person must engage in:

1. **Seeking Knowledge** — through divine revelation and sound reasoning.
2. **Reflecting Deeply** — on the signs within creation and within the soul.
3. **Purifying the Heart** — from pride, doubt, and heedlessness.
4. **Spiritual Struggle** — against ego, desires, and forgetfulness.
5. **Righteous Action** — aligning daily deeds with the higher objectives of Sharia.

4. The Impact of This Understanding on Life

- It rescues the soul from despair, nihilism, and confusion.
- It fills the heart with tranquility, purpose, and dignity.
- It infuses every act with meaning and every moment with direction.
- It empowers the believer to walk their path with resolve and awareness.
- It prepares them to meet God not in fear—but in love, readiness, and light.

"So whoever hopes to meet his Lord, let him do righteous deeds and not associate anyone in the worship of his Lord."
  (Al-Kahf 18:110)

Conclusion: A Final Call to the Wayfarer

Dear seeker,

This journey—mapped from God, to God, with God—now lies before you.

You have been shown your essence, your origin, your mission, and your destiny.

You now hold the compass in your hand:

Faith, Revelation, Intention, Action, and Peace.

So do not let your life slip away in heedlessness or distraction.

Let it be a bridge to eternity, a path walked with devotion, knowledge, and love.

Carry the light of the divine message, and build peace within and around you—

> *"O tranquil soul, return to your Lord, well-pleased and pleasing. Enter among My servants, and enter My Paradise."*
> **(Al-Fajr 89:27–30)**

Encouragement for Active Engagement in the Journey of Faith, Action, and Excellence

Introduction

Knowledge alone does not fulfill its purpose,
  nor does understanding reach its full potential,
  until it is transformed into action—
  until it becomes lived reality.
  Thus, we extend this heartfelt invitation:
  a call to engage in the journey of faith, righteous deeds, and spiritual
excellence (iḥsān).
  A call to make life a conscious walk toward God
  and a mission to uplift the soul and society.

> *"And those who believe and do righteous deeds—those are the companions of Paradise."*
>   (Al-Baqarah 2:82)

1. Why Active Engagement Is Essential

Faith that does not move the limbs is like a tree without fruit.
Action without spiritual excellence is a shell without a soul.
And knowledge without implementation is light left unused in darkness.
The Prophet ﷺ said:

> "Faith has over seventy branches: the highest is saying 'There
> is no god but Allah,' and the lowest is removing harm from the
> road."
> *(Muslim)*

True belief stirs the heart, moves the limbs, and refines the soul.
It urges the person forward on a path of devotion, service, and clarity.

2. Landmarks on the Path of Faith, Action, and Excellence

Each stage of this journey builds upon the next:

1. Faith (Īmān)

A deep-rooted belief in Allah, His angels, His books, His messengers, the
Last Day, and divine decree.
More than acceptance—it is a living conviction that shapes values and
behavior.

2. Righteous Deeds ('Amal Ṣāliḥ)

Acting upon faith through:

• Obligatory duties,
• Avoidance of prohibitions,

• And sincerity in all dealings—public and private.

3. Spiritual Excellence (Iḥsān)

The crown of the journey:
   To worship God as though you see Him—
   And if not, to know with certainty that He sees you.
   This is the heart of integrity, sincerity, and presence with God.

3. How to Embark on the Journey Actively

• Begin each day with a renewed intention: *"Today, I walk toward my Lord."*
• Set realistic, balanced goals: worship, learning, service, and self-discipline.
• Challenge your ego with patience, and reflect regularly on your progress.
• Surround yourself with companions who call you to goodness.
• Stay humble—as you learn, as you act, and as your heart grows.

"And those who strive for Our sake—We will surely guide them to Our paths."
   (Al-ʿAnkabūt 29:69)

4. The Fruits of Practical Commitment

Whoever walks this path will find:

• Light in the heart,
• Peace in the soul,
• Strength in character,

- Blessing in their impact,
- Nearness to God in this life,
- And Paradise in the Hereafter.

> *"Indeed, those who believe and do righteous deeds—We will never let the reward of anyone who did well be lost."*
> (Al-Kahf 18:30)

Conclusion: A Final Invitation

Let this not be where your journey stops—but where it truly begins.
Do not settle for knowledge alone,
nor rest in abstract belief—
but walk toward God with your heart, mind, and hands.
Let your prayer move your limbs.
Let your faith reform your habits.
Let your intention elevate your work.
What step will you take today
to turn belief into action,
and action into excellence?

> *"O tranquil soul, return to your Lord, well-pleased and pleasing."*
> (Al-Fajr 89:27–28)

Inspiration to Live with the Highest Spiritual and Moral Awareness

Introduction

Humanity does not reach its fullness,

    nor does existence fulfill its meaning,

    until a person rises to the highest level of spiritual and moral consciousness—

    a state where deep faith in God,

    freedom from lower desires,

    and the embodiment of noble character

    intertwine in every breath, word, and deed.

> *"And in your own selves—do you not see?"*
> (Adh-Dhariyat 51:21)

1. What Is Spiritual and Moral Awareness?

Spiritual awareness is:

- A living connection to God,
- A heart attuned to His presence,

- A soul striving for nearness through love, surrender, and remembrance.

Moral awareness is:

- The daily practice of virtues—truthfulness, justice, compassion, humility, gratitude, and patience,
- Treating others with dignity, as befits a servant of the Most Merciful.

Together, they form the two wings of inner excellence—one lifting the heart, the other guiding the hands.

2. Why Must We Live with Higher Awareness?

Because without spiritual depth, life becomes mechanical, hollow, and misdirected.

And without moral clarity, behavior becomes impulsive, unjust, or self-serving.

Each soul will one day stand before its Creator, and be asked:

> *"So whoever does an atom's weight of good will see it."*
> (Az-Zalzalah 99:7)

To live with higher awareness is to live with purpose, and to die prepared.

3. Signs of a Life Lived in Awareness

You know a heart is awake when:

- It pauses before every word and act, mindful of God's gaze.
- It seeks purification, not performance.
- It chooses mercy when anger tempts, and truth when silence is safer.
- It reflects on the inevitable return to God.
- It strives to uproot pride, greed, envy, and heedlessness from within.

The Prophet ﷺ said:

> "Be mindful of God wherever you are. Follow a bad deed with a
> good one, and treat people with beautiful character."
>   (*Tirmidhi*)

4. How to Strengthen Your Spiritual and Moral Compass

Make awareness a way of life:

- **Pray** not just with words, but with heart.
- **Remember God (dhikr)** regularly, especially in quiet moments.
- **Read the Qur'an** slowly and intentionally—let it speak to your inner world.
- **Surround yourself** with those who uplift and remind.
- **Hold yourself accountable** before the Day you are held to account.
- **Give generously**, without expecting in return, even if it's only a smile or a prayer.

Every act done with sincerity, no matter how small, becomes a seed in the eternal garden.

5. The Rewards of Living with Awareness

In this world:

- Peace settles into the soul.
- Relationships bloom with integrity and mercy.
- Life takes on weight, direction, and light.

In the next:

- A radiant face,
- A tranquil heart,
- And closeness to the One who created you in love.

"Indeed, the righteous will be in gardens and rivers, in a seat of honor near a Sovereign, Perfect in Ability."
(Al-Qamar 54:54–55)

Conclusion

This is your call:
to live not by impulse, but by illumination.
Not in distraction, but in deliberate devotion.
Let your days be marked by remembrance,
your hands guided by compassion,
and your steps drawn toward the One who awaits you
with mercy beyond measure.
Walk the path with faith in your heart and integrity in your actions—
and the One who is Peace will welcome you
to the *Dar as-Salaam*, the Home of Peace.

Conclusion

From Knowledge to Meaning — From Understanding to the Journey

This book set out to reshape human awareness through a complete, faith-centered worldview—

one that views the human being not as a fleeting biological incident,

but as a moral agent, entrusted with purpose,

accountable for their choices, and destined for eternity.

Together, we traced the foundational truths of existence:

God, creation, the universe, the human soul, life, death, the grave, the Barzakh, resurrection, judgment, Paradise, and Hell.

We then journeyed through the structure of religion—

Islam, Faith (Īmān), and Excellence (Iḥsān)—

before arriving at the seven higher objectives (maqāṣid) of divine law, which preserve both individual dignity and the moral order of society.

But the aim was never just to read.

The aim was to see.

To see life anew—through the lens of purpose.

To turn knowledge into a compass.

To let these truths shape your direction, decisions, and destiny.

This book does not end here.

Its real conclusion lies in what you do next:

- Will you carry forward a deeper consciousness in your everyday life?
- Will you define your identity by your divine purpose, not by society's noise?
- Will you begin your journey to God through love, not mere imitation?
- Will you make faith your personal project, not just a cultural inheritance?

My final word to you:

Do not delay your awakening.
  Do not wait for crisis to ask life's most urgent questions.
  You were not created to consume, compare, and disappear.
  You were created to know.
  To believe.
  To reform.
  To rise.
  Your journey has already begun.
  Choose to walk it—with clarity, courage, and sincerity—
  toward God.

> *"And God invites to the Home of Peace, and guides whom He wills to a straight path."*
>   (Surah Yunus 10:25)

Epilogue

Reflective Conclusion — From the End of the Lines to the Beginning of the Path

The final page is turned,
   but the search does not end.
   For what you've just read is not a conclusion—
   it is a threshold.
   A doorway back to yourself.
   A doorway toward God.
   A call to live with vision, to walk with resolve, and to prepare with awareness.
   You have passed through the great questions:
   Who am I?
   Why was I created?
   What awaits me beyond this life?
   You've journeyed through the eternal truths:
   God, the universe, the soul, life, death, and destiny.
   Now ask yourself—has anything changed in how you see?
   Has the question of your purpose deepened?
   Has your path come into focus?
   The point is not how much you know,
   but what you will do with what you now know.

From a Book to a Life

Take from these pages your provisions.
    Let these meanings shape your direction.
    Let this journey become faith that lives and breathes—
    a light that does not dim.
    Let your life speak your worship.
    Let each moment be a step nearer to the One who gave it.
    Let every breath carry the hope of returning to Him.
    Between your beginning and your end
    is a space of freedom and responsibility—
    a space where God placed you
    to know, to choose, and to rise.

Final Call

Do not delay your repentance.
    Do not dim your awareness.
    Do not wander without purpose.
    Whoever truly knows their Lord will never accept being lost.
    And whoever lives by light will illuminate their path, benefit others,
    and find peace in the depths of their soul.
    Between the words you've read and the choices you now make
    lies the difference between a fleeting life… and an eternal one.

Go forth.

Look back only to learn.
    Pause only to renew your strength.
    And walk on—with love, with certainty, with God.
    He is near.
    The path is open.
    And the ending… is yours to write.

Afterword

Final Word

Now that the chapters of this book have come to a close—
  and the thread has been drawn from creation to destiny,
  from faith to excellence,
  from understanding to purposeful action—
  it is time to pause and reflect.
  Not to end the conversation,
  but to prepare for what comes next.
  This book was written to reconnect what had been scattered,
  to revive clarity where confusion had crept in,
  and to restore the awareness of life's true path and purpose.
  But knowledge alone is not enough.
  Its true value lies in what it inspires.
  What matters now is not what you've read—
  but what you will do with what you've come to know.

Dear Reader…

This is not someone else's story.
  It is yours.
  These pages were meant for you.
  This journey was laid out for your sake.
  These truths were revealed to awaken your soul—
  not to remain theory or words in ink.

You are called to live what you have discovered:
To revisit your heart.
To renew your connection with God.
To become a living expression of truth,
a force for healing, justice, and meaning.

The Invitation

This book ends—
   but your journey begins.
   And every new dawn offers another chance:
   to grow,
   to return,
   to rise.
   So let your life become a message.
   Let your choices speak of awareness.
   Let your moments be filled with purpose.
   And perhaps one day,
   you will write a book like this—
   not with a pen,
   but with a life lived in sincerity and light.

Appendix

A. Summary of the Book's Structure

Part	Title	Theme
1	God, Creation, and the Universe	Foundations of faith and divine origin
2	The Human Being, Birth, and Life	Human identity, purpose, and moral responsibility
3	Death, the Grave, and the Barzakh	Life after death and unseen realities
4	Resurrection and Judgment	Accountability, justice, and eternal fate
5	Hell and Paradise	Consequences of belief and action
6	Islam, Faith (Imān), and Excellence (Iḥsān)	The structure of religion and spiritual development
7	The Seven Higher Objectives of Sharia (Maqāṣid)	Divine law and the flourishing of individual and society
8	The Final Journey	Returning to God with consciousness and purpose

B. Key Qur'anic Verses Referenced

Here is a selection of important Qur'anic verses quoted in the book, organized by theme:

On Creation and Purpose:

"Did you think that We created you in vain and that to Us you would not be returned?" — Al-Mu'minūn 23:115

"I did not create jinn and mankind except to worship Me." — Adh-Dhāriyāt 51:56

On Human Responsibility:

"Indeed, We offered the Trust to the heavens and the earth and the mountains..." — Al-Aḥzāb 33:72

On the Hereafter:

"Whoever is removed from the Fire and admitted to Paradise has indeed succeeded." — Āl ʿImrān 3:185

On Inner Peace:

"Truly, in the remembrance of Allah do hearts find rest." — Ar-Raʿd 13:28

C. Key Hadith Referenced

On Excellence (Iḥsān):

"Iḥsān is to worship Allah as though you see Him..." — *Hadith of Jibrīl (Bukhārī and Muslim)*

On Action and Faith:

"Faith has over seventy branches..." — *Muslim*

On Repentance and Renewal:

"Fear Allah wherever you are, and follow a bad deed with a good one..." — *Tirmidhī*

D. Reflection Questions for the Reader

Personal Awareness:

- Do I truly understand the purpose of my existence? How does this understanding impact my daily life?

Moral Alignment:

- How closely do my values and actions align with the higher objectives of Sharia (religion, life, intellect, lineage, wealth, homeland, and ummah)?

Spiritual Excellence:

- What does "worshiping Allah as though I see Him" mean to me, and how can I cultivate this state?

Practical Action:

- What habits or areas of neglect in my life require transformation in light of this journey?

E. Suggested Further Reading

Classical Works:

- *Al-Muwafaqat* — Imam al-Shāṭibī
- *Iḥyā' 'Ulūm al-Dīn* — Imam al-Ghazālī
- *Madarij al-Sālikīn* — Ibn al-Qayyim

Modern Reflections:

- *In the Early Hours* — Khurram Murad
- *Reclaim Your Heart* — Yasmin Mogahed
- *Purification of the Heart* — Hamza Yusuf

F. Author's Note on Application

The chapters of this book are not meant to be ends in themselves,
   but starting points for real-life transformation.

   Each section can be used for personal journaling, group discussion, or spiritual mentoring sessions.

   I encourage you to revisit the chapters with others, reflect deeply, and walk the journey in community when possible.

About the Author

He is not a graduate of a traditional institution,
  nor a holder of academic degrees in philosophy or Islamic sciences—
  but a lifelong student on the path of meaning and reflection.
  His learning was self-guided, fueled by sincerity, perseverance, and a
deep yearning for truth.
  He was never content with superficial answers or cultural clichés.
  Instead, he immersed himself in the Qur'an, classical texts, and
philosophy—
  reading with the mind, reflecting with the heart, and walking alongside
scholars through their words before ever meeting them in person.
  He believes that true education begins with reading the self,
  and that the journey of the human being cannot be complete without
  reason, fitrah (innate nature), and revelation—
  each guiding the other toward wholeness and awakening.
  He does not claim completion, nor does he seek fame.
  He writes as he searches, teaches as he learns,
  and offers this book as the distilled fruit of years of reading, reflection,
and striving.
  Through this work, he hopes to open doors for others—
  doors he often approached alone and in silence—

and to contribute, in whatever small way,

to a spiritual and intellectual revival rooted in sincerity, meaning, and return to God.

You can connect with me on:

🌐 https://www.abdellatifraji.com

Subscribe to my newsletter:

✉ https://www.thehumanjourney.info

www.ingramcontent.com/pod-product-compliance
Lightning Source LLC
LaVergne TN
LVHW052013080426
835513LV00018B/2021